KT-568-783

OLD ENGLISH FURNITURE

CHEST OF DRAWERS IN CARVED MAHOGANY (CHIPPENDALE)
(*circa* 1760)

Frontispiece

HAMPDEN GORDON, C.B.

Old English Furniture

A SIMPLE GUIDE

LONDON
JOHN MURRAY
50 ALBEMARLE STREET, W1.

First Edition July 1948
Reprinted September 1948
Reprinted January 1959

Made and printed in Great Britain by
Butler & Tanner Ltd., Frome and London
and published by John Murray (Publishers) Ltd.

Contents

Contents

List of Illustrations

List of Illustrations

The illustrations, except where otherwise stated are by courtesy of The Victoria and Albert Museum. Crown Copyright Reserved.

* *By courtesy of 'Country Life'.*

§ *By courtesy of H. J. C. Mackarness, Esq.*

† *From author's collection.*

The Aim of this Book

This book is not written for those who already know all that there is to be known about the meaning of the term 'bolection mouldings' or who are prepared to argue the disputed point of the date of Hepplewhite's earliest work or the year in which Sheraton first came to London. It is written primarily for the 'man in the street'.

The average person who possesses a leaning towards old furniture and would like very much to know something about it, is apt to be discouraged by the mass of detail which a knowledge of the subject appears to involve, by the technical terms that he is assumed to understand, and by the difficulties that are supposed to beset the collector. It is true that for the purposes of the first-class expert the intricacy and the problems are real enough, for the ultimate interest of the connoisseur lies largely in the subtle points that distinguish the exceptional piece. For the purposes of the average collector the situation is different. He must know how to recognise Period styles; he must know where particular difficulties lie and be aware of the traps that he has to avoid; but the wealth of detail on fine points which the first-class expert must know and weigh is not essential to a working knowledge of the subject.

Many busy people would like to possess this working knowledge—for good reasons. The subject is attractive from three points of view: the artistic, the romantic, and also the practical. From the practical angle a piece of genuine antique furniture is, apart from its use, a sound investment, and a second world-war has increased its value.

Its romantic appeal is to those who, both in this country and in America, cling to the reminders of the English heritage in the manners and fashions of bygone days. There is a glamour about the past that can never wholly be 'de-bunked.' The third angle, the artistic, is the most important of the three; for neither rarity-value nor historical associations are a substitute for beauty.

To anyone who has an eye for beauty of line and grace of proportion the miscellaneous array of chairs and cabinets, chests and sideboards which are labelled 'antiques' in many shops, can only afford a depressing experience. Much of it is likely to be of poor quality, second-rate workmanship and doubtful antecedents; much of it, even if it be genuinely old, will nevertheless be definitely ugly. There are, of course, people to whom anything 'antique' possesses an attraction just because it is old and apart from the question whether or not it has qualities of beauty. To others it will not be desirable at all unless it is also a thing of beauty. To maintain that all Period furniture is beautiful would certainly be an exaggeration; but the bulk of it displays these characteristics of line and proportion and artistry of decoration by which English furniture of the 18th century achieved a great name in the history of the crafts. In judging the merits of old English furniture artistic perception is all-important.

This book is intended for the busy person who, faced with a piece of 'antique' furniture, wants to know just what it purports to be, to what Period and style it belongs, and what he must do to be able to judge whether it is really the genuine thing. There are also gaps in existing knowledge of historical fact of which the collector ought at least to be aware, and some points that have caused high debate among experts. The attempt here made is to give the reader the essential points, with a sketch of their setting in social history, in a short form and as simply as possible.

H.G.

CHAPTER I

The Modern Approach

In this age of standardisation and machine-made products the appeal of individual examples of careful and artistic craftsmanship, whether 'old' or new, is growing; and so is their value. There is increasing appreciation, too, of the truth that the lasting comfort of a room depends a great deal on proportion and line, and that a few pieces of furniture of good design, arranged with an eye to balance and harmony, are far more restful in their effect than a jumble of articles, each severally designed for comfort and convenience, which fail to combine in a well-balanced whole. There is no doubt about the fact that the majority of the English furniture of the 17th and 18th centuries possessed those qualities of line, proportion and, generally speaking, restraint in decoration that contribute directly to that subtle sense of repose which is the secret of the successful furnishing of a room.

The old furniture which interests the average collector is not the 'museum piece' which is beyond his purse, but the chair or bookcase or mirror which could find a place in his home. With such a purpose in mind he requires a working knowledge of the subject. He wishes first, perhaps, to be able to tell whether the chest or table with which he is confronted is a genuine antique, or a reproduction, or a fake which is not what it pretends to be. He desires, secondly, to be able to tell to what Period the piece belongs (assuming it to be genuine) and at what approximate date it was made; and, further, if it is a product of the 18th century, or rather that part of the 18th century when styles are named after famous designers such as Chippendale, Hepplewhite, Sheraton and so on, he needs to know to what particular style it belongs. This amount of knowledge is still required even if he is content with a good reproduction, because he wishes to be sure that the thing that he is buying reproduces the merits, correctly and faithfully, of the original design.

These, then, are the two objectives at which a working knowledge should aim; and a working knowledge of this kind is within the reach of every person who is willing to take a sufficient interest.

In practice the second of the two objectives is the one that has to be tackled first. The collector has first to acquire the knowledge by which he may know what a given piece is—or rather what it purports to be—as to Period, style and approximate date. At first sight the progress of modern study appears to have added to the difficulty of the task, for it is a popular pastime of modern days to 'de-bunk' the cherished beliefs of our grandfathers. Even forty years ago most people were aware that to call a chair a 'Chippendale' chair did not mean that it was made by Thomas Chippendale; if only for the reason that the Chippendale workshops, even if they were not very small (there is no real evidence to settle this point), could not have produced the mass of furniture that posthumous fame has attributed to them. It was recognised quite a long time ago that a large number of designers and makers were in flourishing business at the same dates as the few whose names have become renowned, and that all designs were freely borrowed. Since then, however, painstaking research has thrown fresh doubts on past beliefs. It has suggested that Chippendale was not responsible for more than a fraction of the designs in his book. It has pointed to the gaps in existing knowledge concerning others of the famous designers—the facts that are missing about George Hepplewhite or disputed dates in the case of Sheraton. It has emphasised the absence of positive proof that a single piece of existing furniture can actually be ascribed to these two designers.

Points such as these are extremely interesting to those who are making an intensive study of 18th century furniture-design. To the new collector they are confusing, and are also largely irrelevant issues. The study of the facts, so far as they are known, has not 'de-bunked' the great names. It has not shed doubt on the cardinal fact that the skill and personality of Thomas Chippendale, George Hepplewhite, the Adam brothers and Thomas Sheraton established, in each case, a definite style. It is true that at certain periods and dates an intriguing criss-cross of styles occurs which presents subtle problems to the connoisseur; but this does not alter the general position. The task of the average collector is eased, not aggravated, by modern research. In the absence of documentary proof, such as the existence of original bills or trade labels, he cannot say, nor can anyone else, that this chair or that table was the work of a named cabinet maker; but he is able to tell, if he takes the trouble, whether the chair or cabinet or chest conforms to a known and distinctive style, and, if it does, what style that is, and to what approximate date it belongs. To attain this knowledge is the first step, and modern research has assisted the student. Briefly, it has defined the limits of what it is possible for him to know without the possession of second-sight. It has cleared the air for concentration on styles rather than on individual accomplishment.

The task of the first-class expert is different. He is rarely concerned with a piece of furniture of normal style and average quality. His judgment is required on fine points where the verdict given by expert opinion may make a big difference in market value; and such an assessment, in a given case, can be an extremely subtle matter. Two Queen Anne cabinets, to take an example, both equally genuine and in equal condition, may differ in value by large sums. Points which will only be given due weight by someone possessing a wide experience may render the one unusual and rare, while the other is only an excellent specimen which has no claim to 'museum' interest. A cabinet-bookcase of 1780 may raise a most difficult question of style, as the reader of Chapter 9 will observe, if the expert is pressed to be extremely precise. Indeed, if the first-class expert claims that his work requires a life-time of study, some practical experience of cabinet-making, a detailed knowledge of the woods used, and a long experience in the actual handling of fine examples of Period furniture—if he claims that all these things are needed in order to possess his qualifications, no sensible person will challenge the statement. But the ordinary collector is not so placed. He requires, it is true, some knowledge and experience, but not the degree of knowledge and experience essential to the connoisseur. At the same time he can go a long way, for, by knowing the points that distinguish each style, he can recognise in a great many cases the special features that make a piece rare.

The background of the subject is social history, and the span of time which concerns the collector extends from the year 1500 to 1800 or 1820. As social conditions in England changed, so furniture changed in kind, in quantity, in quality and in style. A simple illustration is the well-known instance of the rail or 'stretcher' which joined the four legs of the Tudor chair. In the early part of the 16th century the total population of the country was small—little more than four million people; very little furniture existed at all except in the homes of the wealthy families; there were no carpets to cover the floors, and the rushes which were used in place of carpets became dirty and damp. Chairs were confined to important people (ordinary folk sat on long stools) and the stretchers of the chairs, placed close to the floor, provided a means of keeping the feet from the damp and filth of the rush-strewn floor. Later in the century a change occurs. The standard of domestic comfort had risen; carpets were taking the place of rushes (at least where important people were seated) and the stretcher which joins the front legs of the early 17th century chair no longer always runs close to the floor but is often placed much higher up. It has ceased to be purely utilitarian and is sometimes treated with carved decoration. This, of course, is only a trivial example of social conditions affecting design; but bigger events had larger results. Obvious cases are the Civil War with its introduction of Puritan modes; the great re-action in manners and style when the 'Merry Monarch' came to the throne; or the importation by William and Mary of Dutch ideas and Dutch craftsmen. Foreign events had effects, too; as witness the influence on Georgian design of the glamorous fashions of the French court in the middle years of the 18th century, or the advent of the 'English Empire' style as a direct result of the curious pseudo-classic vogue that was born out of the French Revolution. The close link between furniture design and the social and political developments of the times is an added reason for the first step which a working knowledge of the subject demands. That step is to form a clear idea of the general framework of dates and events that divide the whole subject into compartments—the 'Periods' of English style.

At one time a popular method of approach was to divide the centuries (1500 to 1800) into four Periods of English furniture by reference to the woods used. It was possible to speak of an Age of Oak from 1500 to 1660; an Age of Walnut from the Restoration up to the end of Queen Anne's reign; an Age of Mahogany from 1715 up to about the year 1770; and a Satinwood or Composite Age from 1770 to

1800. Such a classification is most misleading, and the modern approach is more accurate. Probably the division into main Periods which is most helpful as a general picture is the following:—

I. The Tudor period, which includes the Elizabethan style (roughly 1500 to 1600).
II. The Stuart period, which includes the Jacobean*, Commonwealth and Restoration styles (1603 to 1688).
III. The period of Dutch influence. (William and Mary, and Queen Anne: 1689 to 1714).
IV. The Georgian period, which has to be considered by reference to styles of its famous designers, (1714 to 1820).

Each Period marks great changes in fashion in accordance with the trend of social conditions, and each of them calls for separate study, but an outline-knowledge of the order of events is an absolute essential to every collector. The background has to be seen as a whole.

*'Jacobean' is used in a conventional sense for the style of the first two Stuart kings, James I and Charles I.

CHAPTER 2

A Sketch of the Background

THE newcomer to the subject who plunges straight into detailed descriptions of the Period styles is apt to meet terms and allusions that are confusing. He finds, for example, that one era is described as 'the great period of English inlay,' only to be told at a much later stage that 'inlaid work was now the new fashion.' In the time of Queen Anne he finds that 'japanning' was the latest craze in artistic circles; but again towards the end of the 18th century he is told that 'japanning was the new vogue.' He discovers that the term 'Regency style' crops up in the early 18th century when a regent was ruling for the young King of France, and again in the early 19th century in the glittering days of the Prince Regent who afterwards became King George IV. He encounters constant references to French influence on English design, but cannot visualise what this influence means in terms of design unless he knows something of the style of decoration employed in France at the relevant date. Points like this may be simple enough when explained, but perhaps it is as well not to take it for granted that the reader is familiar with all the terms used in accounts of this subject or needs no reminder of the dates and events that go to make up the historical background.

The two uses of the term 'japanning' will be explained in their place, but 'inlay' and 'marquetry' occur so often that a note in advance may be useful. In the inlay of Tudor and Stuart times the surface decorated was normally of solid wood. The design was built into this solid surface in thin small pieces of other woods or of ivory, bone or mother-of-pearl In the William and Mary and Queen Anne period the surface to be decorated was not solid wood but normally a veneer or thin layer of walnut, and the inlaid work was a process of inserting one veneer which was cut with a saw into another veneer which formed the ground. This was a process similar to that employed in France by Boulle, whose work in tortoiseshell and brass has left us the technical name 'Buhl,' and also by the other famous designers of the Louis Quatorze and Louis Quinze periods whose styles are sketched in Chapter 11; and the French word 'marqueterie' is always applied to the inlay of these French designers and also to the fine and elaborate work of the William and Mary and Queen Anne reigns. In England there was a long gap between this 'marquetry' of Queen Anne days and the inlaid work of Sheraton's time towards the close of the 18th century. This later work was of both kinds; but whether it consisted of satinwood lines inlaid in a solid mahogany ground or was itself a veneer set in a veneer, as in floral designs on a satinwood table, it is always referred to simply as 'inlay.' Thus 'inlay' is the generic term, and 'marquetry' is a special kind of inlay, and the name 'marquetry' is confined by custom to the work of the famous French ébénistes and to the inlaid work of the walnut era.

Many words used in describing furniture are borrowed from the language of architecture, and a few of them may be worth recalling. In the secretaire shown on page 46 the 'cornice' (or crown) is the projecting moulding which forms the topmost line of all, and the 'frieze' is the long broad band below it. In this particular case the face of the frieze is rounded in shape and the technical word for this shaping is 'ovolo.' 'Pediment' is the architectural name for a shaped decoration which crowns a cornice. It usually takes the form of a triangle, and a 'broken pediment' is the more complex form in which the top of the triangle is broken by a gap. In 18th century cabinets and book-cases pediments, as distinct from straight-line tops, were a very frequent feature of design. A 'patera' is a small decorated ornament which frequently appears in classical friezes and was much used by the Adam brothers either in friezes or at the top of legs. In furniture it is generally round or oval and is decorated with pointed leaves which converge on a small bead in the middle.

'Ogee' is a technical term which refers to a shape often seen in mouldings and sometimes in the bracket design of foot used as a support for heavy pieces such as cabinets and chests-of-drawers. The feet of the secretaire shown in the photograph (page 46) are bracket feet of ordinary form; but the 'ogee' is a curve that suggests an 'S', and an ogee bracket curves to the ground in a shape suggesting a short bent knee. The ogee bracket was used by Chippendale as a support for pieces of fine quality (see photograph on page 82), and it has to be distinguished from the 'French' foot which was very much favoured by Hepplewhite and is seen in the photograph on page 101.

Three other technical words worth noting are 'cusp', 'arabesques' and 'baluster', all of which occur frequently in books on the subject of furniture or decoration. In architecture a 'cusp' is a projecting point on the under-surface of a Gothic arch. In furniture it appears frequently in pseudo-Gothic decoration, and 'cusp' is specially used for the small turned ornament that is often suspended from the arches in the under-framing of Queen Anne tables and stands for cabinets or chests-of-drawers. 'Arabesques' is a more important word and refers to a type of conventional decoration that was borrowed from Italy and was used by designers from the time of Queen Elizabeth onwards. Arabesque work is usually described as a design made up of 'foliated scrolls': it consists of a network of light curved sprays, and is seen at its best in some of the intricate marquetry of the Queen Anne era as shown in the photograph on page 140. A 'baluster' (or banister) is a small pillar. Adaptations of the baluster form are seen in the backs of the chairs shown on page 38, but 'baluster leg' is used with special reference to a slim leg that was popular in the Period of Dutch Influence in combination with a flat or moulded stretcher, and was either turned or was flat-cut on its six faces and tapered.

. . . .

As regards the general historical background the following is an attempt to give 'a bird's eye view' of the order of events through the four Periods.

The English furniture of the 18th century forms the chief interest of most collectors, from the beautiful walnut of Queen Anne's day to the styles attributed to the great designers of 1750 to 1800. This is naturally the case in the light of the facts, for the great majority of the articles of furniture which are associated with ideas of comfort either did not exist, or did not come into general use, until nearly the end of the 17th century. There exists, however, a large amount of the oak and walnut of the 17th century, for in the latter part of the Tudor period and during the whole of the 17th century, it was common practice to oil, wax and polish the furniture, so that it had a good chance of surviving. This was not true generally of the oak furniture of earlier times.

The first of the divisions, the Tudor Period, covers approximately the hundred years from 1500 to 1600, the first half of which coincides roughly with the reign of Henry VIII and the second half with the reign of Elizabeth; and outside a number of ancient houses, public museums and private collections very little indeed exists to-day of the domestic furniture of those times. This being the case, its interest to the collector centres mainly in its design, for its ornamentation in deep carving and an early form of inlaid-work shows the mediæval or 'Gothic' style being superseded by the new influence that had spread gradually over western Europe—the rebirth of classical teaching. From this blending of the old monastic with the new and more free 'Renaissance' manner an English style began to emerge, and two events were contributing causes to a general advance in the arts and crafts—the rise in wealth of the merchant classes, and later, in 1572, the massacres of St. Bartholomew's Eve. Prosperity raised the standard of comfort, which hitherto had been very low, and the persecution of the French Huguenots resulted in the settlement in this country of large numbers of skilled artisans. The style which emerged was distinctive enough to be given the name 'Elizabethan', and the Tudor furniture which survives to-day normally dates from the reign of Elizabeth. As a rule it possesses well-marked characteristics that distinguish it from the early Stuart style which followed. The wood used was mainly oak.

The Stuart Period, taken as a whole (1603–1688), saw a great increase in the quantity of furniture made and a marked advance in the types introduced. The dawn of comfort has arrived at last in the homes of the yeoman class, and a large amount of plain furniture was now produced all over the country. King Charles I, too, was a patron of art, and an ardent and cultured collector whose personal example did a great deal to encourage interest in the crafts and taste in furnishing. The Period as a whole falls into two main phases divided by the years of the Commonwealth régime.

The two reigns of the first phase (James I and Charles I) are conveniently classed as 'Jacobean', to distinguish the style of this half of the century from the great change in the second half. This was the age when plain panelling framed in simple mouldings largely supplanted carved decoration; when drawers in furniture were introduced; when chairs began to be in common use; and when light and easily movable articles, such as the gate-leg table, appeared. Incidentally, it was also the time when the first English furniture went to America. A quantity of the finer furniture, both Jacobean and Elizabethan, disappeared as a result of the Civil War and the Puritan anti-royalist zeal. The contents of twenty or more great houses are said to have been destroyed in those years. But the simpler models, particularly those of the farmstead type such as dressers and settles, survived these perils, and much of this 'old oak' still exists.

Then came the short-lived Commonwealth era when the Puritan hatred of Cavalier modes had a damping effect on the progress of the crafts. It left no particular mark on design, if we except the so-called Cromwellian chair, but it had great results, by way of reaction, on the succeeding Restoration style.

A notable change came in 1660 when Charles II assumed the throne. The émigré party had sojourned during their exile in France where the splendour of the court of Louis XIV was in striking contrast to anything known to English 17th century design. Continental influence on fashion was strong, and taste underwent a great change. The use of walnut became the vogue; caning supplanted solid wood for the seats and backs of chairs and 'day-beds'; pierced carving gave an added lightness; and the furniture of the Restoration, in a great reaction from Puritan manners, achieved a new and decorative style. From the point of view of the arts and crafts several public events had a special importance. The great fire of 1666, which destroyed a large part of the City of London, spread the 'classic' influence of Sir

Christopher Wren, who had followed the lead of Inigo Jones, on the general style of English building, and it was largely due to the help of Wren that carving received a great impetus from the marvellous work of Grinling Gibbons. The crafts were also considerably assisted by a second influx of Protestant refugees, including a large number of skilled workmen, which followed from French political action (the revocation of the Edict of Nantes) in the year 1685. At the same time trade with the East was increasing, and the importation of Chinese porcelain, and also of oriental lacquer, created demands for new types of production. Inlaid work enjoyed a revival, and, broadly speaking, Restoration furniture was gay and attractive in its decoration and a great advance on the Jacobean.

With the forced retirement of James II in 1688 the stage was set for a new era not only in Parliamentary control but in design and manners generally.

William and Mary were followed to this country by large numbers of Dutch craftsmen, and the ensuing Period of Dutch Influence culminated in the 'Queen Anne style' of the opening years of the 18th century. The change of style was gradual, of course, and the furniture of the reign of William and Mary possesses a special interest for the collector in showing clearly the process of transition from the late-Stuart to the new ideas. The straight-line character of previous design is seen in this William and Mary furniture making way for an era of plain curves. It was a phase distinguished by marquetry-work on veneered walnut of an intricate and fine type of which the Dutch were the pioneers, and by the emergence, at first in a disguised form, of that famous feature the cabriole leg, seen in the chair on page 51. The fully perfected Queen Anne style was more sober in its decoration. Its best known features are the cabriole leg and the plain hooped back of the Queen Anne chair.

This period of Dutch Influence has always appealed to

collectors strongly. It is the period, *par excellence*, of walnut-wood. The Queen Anne style was quiet and homely, and the standard of comfort showed a great advance. Many new types of furniture made their appearance such as the card-table proper and the writing-bureau, while articles such as mirrors and clocks were no longer confined to the wealthy classes. Court cupboards and chests became things of the past with the advent, in London, of smaller rooms. The influence of architecture was strong. Great attention was paid to interior decoration as a united whole, and the Queen Anne style made a name in building. It was also the chief period of English Lacquer. The making of lacquer in this country in clever imitation of the oriental made great progress under Dutch tuition, and enjoyed a temporary and fitful vogue.

Queen Anne died in 1714, and the fourth Period is the Georgian era (1715 to 1820) which for the sake of convenience and clearness has to be studied in several compartments. (These compartments do not correspond with the dates of the reigns, which are George I, 1715 to 1727, George II 1727 to 1760, George III 1760 to 1820).

The introduction of mahogany as the fashionable wood soon after George I came to the throne created in itself a new era, and the first thirty years after that date was a transitional phase when Queen Anne tradition still governed design but walnut was gradually superseded in favour by the new wood. At the same time there was a change in taste: plain designs were elaborated, architectural details were much in evidence in bureau-cabinets and similar pieces, and furniture took on a heavy tone. Marquetry-work went out of fashion in company with the vogue of walnut. Mahogany lent itself to carving. No great designers had yet appeared to lead the fashion into new channels and create specific styles of their own, and the furniture of this interim period must be classed in the mass as 'Early Georgian'; but the combination of Queen Anne tradition with the use of mahogany and a ponderous taste gave it characteristics easy to recognise. In France, too, design was changing. The death of the 'grande monarque' brought an end to the stately 'Louis Quatorze' style, and the regency of the Duke of Orleans laid the foundations of the Louis Quinze style in a lighter but more extravagant vein.

In the latter part of the reign of George II (1727 to 1760) the era begins when styles are named after famous designers. In the second half of the 18th century, although social distinctions were extremely rigid and the whole culture was highly artificial, personality was able to make its mark in literature and all forms of art, and the craft of cabinet-making flourished. But fashion in furniture, as in building and dress, was subject to constant and sudden changes, and ambitious designers were apt to be swayed by the latest craze of the fashionable world. It was in such a vortex of shifting currents that Thomas Chippendale rose to the surface and a new direction was given to design.

From this time onward the study of furniture is the study of the style of particular men and the schools of craftsmen who followed their lead. The first is the style of Chippendale, the second the style of the Adam brothers (the famous partnership called 'the Adelphi'), the third is attributed, rightly or wrongly, to the early work of George Hepplewhite, and the fourth is a new and composite style that dates from about the year 1770 when satinwood was coming into general use and painted furniture started its vogue. In the last decade of the 18th century the great name in the sphere of design is Thomas Sheraton.

Each of these styles is a study in itself. To some extent they intermingled, but as soon as the influence of Chippendale had waned the general trend up to 1800 was a movement away from carved mahogany towards still lighter ideas in design and new conceptions of decoration. There was, first, a revived architectural influence, the 'classic' manner in a fresh form as interpreted by the Adam brothers, and then a revival of inlaid work often described as 'the second period of English inlay' but quite distinct in its style and its woods from the marquetry of the Dutch era. The painted furniture that came into vogue was a natural result of the change in taste that was taking place in France as well as in this country. Daintiness of form and colour was the aim of design in both countries from the 1770's to the close of the century, and the new French style of Louis Seize had considerable effect on English line.

This 'golden era' of the famous designers from Chippendale to Sheraton is naturally a complex picture on account of its sequence of swift changes. It starts in a phase of heavy furniture, carved mahogany and the cabriole leg and ends in a phase of small light pieces, dainty decoration and slim straight legs. In addition it was prolific in types: there is hardly an article of useful furniture that had not evolved by the year 1800. Incidentally, it was also the period when English porcelain was first made. The earliest products of Bow and Chelsea date from just before 1750, and these factories were followed within a few years by Bristol, Longton-Hall, Worcester and Derby. Wedgwood 'Jasper' ware, especially famous in connection with Adam decoration, did not appear until 1775.

The fifth and last phase of the Georgian Period (1800 to 1820) presents, once more, a complete contrast. The 'golden era of English furniture' is regarded as ending with the turn of the century, and certainly Sheraton's latest designs, published in 1803. show little signs of his earlier taste. A large section of fashion was led at this time by the future Prince Regent, who was afterwards to be George IV, and it is evident that the Prince's party was all-powerful in the lead which it gave to design. In striking distinction from the delicate manner that had run parallel, in this country, to the elegancies of the court of Louis XVI and Marie Antoinette, the Regency style was flamboyant alike in form and in colour. In France the violent political changes following on the Revolution had resulted in a new republican style which avoided all traces of the *ancien régime*—a pseudo-classical and virile style which came to be known as 'French Empire'. In spite of the war between the two countries the classical elements in the new French fashion form a marked feature of the Regency style, and the final production of the Georgian Period is the furniture since called 'English Empire'.

. . . . . .

For the convenience of the reader a brief survey of the main French styles from Louis Quatorze to French Empire is given in a separate chapter (page 125), and the minor English makers and designers whose names at least should be known to the collector, such as William Vile, Gillow, Ince and Mayhew and Shearer, are listed in Chapter 12.

A short note is included in Chapter 13 on the furniture of English origin or type that is called in America 'Old Colonial'.

The presence of the original handles and lock-plates (which were often replaced) adds to the value of Period furniture. A short note on the main types is also included in Chapter 13.

CHAPTER 3

The Tudor Period

In the century preceding the year 1500 design in this country was governed by the style known as Gothic, and the resultant decoration in architecture and in such furniture as was used at this time is seen in the form of the 'tracery' stonework that divided the pointed windows of churches and in the panelling known as 'linen-fold' which is based on the shape of a folded napkin. This mediæval 'Gothic' style was much modified by the Renaissance movement which, starting in Italy in the 15th century, spread over Europe and began to affect English furniture-design at the beginning of the Tudor reigns. Just as in thought and in learning, the Renaissance movement was a break-away from mediæval tradition, so in art it was a revival of the Classic manner, which was far more free in its inspiration. The Classical leavening of Gothic design is illustrated in the case of furniture by the introduction into carved ornament of arches and columns, by medallions containing portrait-heads, and, generally speaking, by a type of design in which it can be seen that the artist at work is no longer so closely bound by the monastic tradition of the Middle Ages. King Henry VII (1485 to 1509) had imported Italian artists into England, and the year 1500 was roughly the date when this new influence began to affect the decoration of English furniture.

As already mentioned, there is very little furniture of the earlier phase of the Tudor Period which the modern collector is able to acquire; and this statement is only slightly less true of the second or 'Elizabethan' phase. The collector, as distinct from the student of design, may not think it to be of any great interest. The 'old oak' beloved of collectors is normally the oak of the next century. Some knowledge, however, of the characteristics of the furniture of Tudor times is necessary to an understanding of the 'marks' that distinguish the next period. These characteristics can be stated briefly.

In the time of King Henry VIII the types of furniture were few in number and were limited to the wealthy class. They were tables and stools of the trestle type, box-like chairs, chests for storage, four-poster beds, and various kinds of 'buffets' used for the display of food or cupboards used for containing it. These possessions were normally built of oak, and by modern standards were heavy and clumsy. It would be a mistake, however, to picture the houses of the early Tudor nobles as gloomy and sombre in general effect. They may have been lacking in sanitation: they were not lacking in warm colours. The furniture was often 'picked-out' with paint; and the age was one in which rich silk damasks and velvets woven in bright hues and fine tapestries were much in vogue. The general standard of comfort was rising, and the King had reasons for encouraging this trend which were partly private and partly political. For one thing, the young King Henry VIII was himself interested in the fine arts and brought to this country a number of artists such as Holbein and Torrigiano. Another personal motive was envy: the King was jealous of the splendid chateaux of his rival Francis I of France. Further, it was a matter of policy to promote prosperity among the middle class of 'small gentry' and burgesses as a counterbalance to the great nobles. As a result there was much progress; and even in the first half of the century a distinctively English style was arising as regards the carved decoration of furniture. In the pieces preserved in various collections the

AN ELIZABETHAN BUFFET

blending of Renaissance 'classic' detail with the old Gothic can be seen clearly.

In Elizabeth's time this style had 'arrived', and since a certain amount of this furniture is extant, at any rate for the purpose of study, its characteristics are well known. In the main the wood employed was oak. To suppose that walnut was not used at all in Tudor times is incorrect; but the majority of the tables, cupboards and so on were solid pieces built in oak. Other woods were used for inlaid work, but it was not until the days of Drake and Raleigh that this decoration was widely used, and even then it was markedly crude, though some fine specimens are known, such as the famous Bess of Hardwick's table of 1568 at Hardwick Hall. Geometrical or floral patterns in small pieces of cherry, yew, holly or pear, which were often stained, were the usual themes —a bouquet of flowers in a vase or basket, or a chequered band in contrasted woods. The slices of wood were considerably thicker than the fine veneers of a hundred years later. In carving, typical Elizabethan designs are the flowing patterns known as 'arabesques' suggestive of sprays of slender foliage, and bands of the so-called 'strap' decoration in which straps or ribbons are interlaced. Heraldic devices are frequently introduced, and grotesque figures and masks are common. But the most noticeable feature in Elizabethan decoration is the bulbous swell resembling a pomegranate which was boldly carved on the legs of tables, on the pillars of the great four-poster beds and on the short columns that support the tiers of the 'buffet' and the 'court cupboard'. This feature is shown in the photograph of a buffet on page 20.

The buffet illustrated is an exceptional piece in as much as it is made of walnut. It shows the typical style of carving and chequer inlay in holly and bog-oak.

There were four main kinds of cupboard in use, the names of which are often confused. The 'court cupboard' was the latest of these: the others are the 'buffet', the 'hutch' and the 'armoire'. They were all flat-topped rectangular pieces which originated from the everyday need for storage space for armour and food. The 'hutch' was a mediæval model: a small cupboard standing on legs, of a simple and elementary design. A 'double hutch' was merely taller, and might be five feet high or so. The 'armoire' was a large piece—the predecessor of the modern wardrobe. Originally a simple cupboard for storage, the ornamentation of later specimens shows that it came to be highly prized as a piece of decorative household furniture. This was also the case with the 'buffet', the forerunner of the later side-table and sideboard. Early 'buffets' were long low cupboards on legs, but this model developed later on, when plate and pewter were much in evidence, to something resembling a 'dinner wagon'. The photograph shows an Elizabethan model built in the form of open tiers. The early cupboards of all types were often pierced to admit air: they were used to store the 'livery' rations which were handed out to retainers and servants. Small 'hutches' used for this purpose are often described as 'dole cupboards'. All the earlier models are rare.

The 'court cupboard' is quite distinct. It appeared in Elizabethan times, but remained a popular and prized form for at least a hundred years or more. It was normally built in two storeys, but a three-decker model is also found; and its upper part is always 'recessed'. The latter feature, which is quite distinctive, is best explained by a photograph. The specimen shown on page 26 is later than Elizabethan and belongs to the Jacobean era, but the differences lie in detail only, not in the general line and build. A point to notice is that the old cupboards originally stood on feet.

Elizabethan tables and stools showed a great advance in design and construction on the mediæval trestle form. The new form was the framed type, in which the trestle was superseded by legs joined by long stretcher-rails close to the floor, and the legs were adorned by deep carving. There was also the so-called 'draw' table which embodied a very ingenious arrangement. Two leaves were inserted under the top which could be pulled out at either end, the top proper falling into place. Chairs remained uncommon throughout this period. The standard Elizabethan arm-chair was not boxed-in like the early Tudor type, but it remained a heavy chair of stiff rectangular form, with typical carving on its panelled back, a plain seat of solid oak and carved front-legs and arm-supports. A change in Elizabethan days was the introduction of cushions ('quysshons'). Lighter types of chair are very rare. One was the old-fashioned turned or 'thrown' chair of which the frame consisted of thick turned rails. In France this turned type of chair was certainly as early as the 12th century. Another light type is known as the 'double X' shape, in which the arms form the upper part of the X and the legs the lower—a design based on a type of construction which was used by the ancient civilisations and is also called the 'curule' form.

Viewing the work of the period as a whole, as far as decorative furniture is concerned, the great possessions of the Tudor household were the four-poster beds, the armoires and buffets, the large tables and the court-cupboards. Genuine Tudor pieces are hard to acquire. Extant specimens of the finest furniture either remain in their original homes or have found their way into scattered collections. The collector of 16th century oak has to rest content with the smaller pieces—the chests of the ordinary coffer type, which are marked by the style of their carving or inlay and their very simple method of construction; the small 'joyn'd' stools known as 'coffin stools'; and the boxes made to hold books or papers which are generally described as 'bible boxes'. These chests and boxes and 'joyn'd' stools continued to be made in the Stuart period, but the carving and style of the next century were generally distinct from the Tudor manner and the changes set out in the next Chapter are usually marked sufficiently clearly as to indicate the later date. Dates carved on the boxes or chests are not in themselves a safe guide: they were often added in later days.

From the point of view of craftsmanship the second half of the 16th century brought a marked advance, though the methods used and the tools available were still of an extremely simple kind. The parts of tables, cupboards, and the rest were pegged together with wooden pins. The inlaid work was generally of a crude type, but the carved decoration was vigorous and deep. Fixed upholstery was unknown, but tapestries and richly woven rugs or carpets were employed as covers for tables and buffets, and had been so used from early times. The furniture was honest and dignified. The work of this age, as of any other, demands, for its fullest appreciation, to be seen in the setting for which it was intended. Imagination has to reconstruct the long low rooms of the great houses with their bay-windows reaching to the ceiling, the finely moulded plaster above, and the panelled oak that covered the walls. The Elizabethans knew how to build.

CHAPTER 4

The Stuart Period

TUDOR furniture was of straight-line design; and this is broadly true of the furniture made up to the close of the next century. In other respects the dawn of the 17th century ushered in a new era in the furnishing of the English home.

In matters of decoration the period was split in half by the revolt against gaiety and extravagance that accompanied the dominance of the Puritan influence under the Commonwealth (1649 to 1660). As a result there are two distinct phases of style to consider, divided by the short Cromwellian decade of plain-models: first, the phase from the opening years of the century up to the Civil War—which may conveniently be called Jacobean; and, subsequently, the Restoration furniture of 1660–1688. The points of difference between typical Jacobean and typical Restoration furniture are very marked.

JACOBEAN

Fashion did not, of course, change abruptly with the accession of James 1st in 1603; but it is clear that the demand for comfort and for small-house furniture was spreading rapidly throughout the country. There is a general lightening of construction and design, well seen in the legs of tables and the 'pillars' supporting the canopy of court-cupboards where the exaggerated 'bulb' ornament of

MID-17TH CENTURY COURT CUPBOARD

Elizabethan fashion gives place to a more slender turned swell (see the illustration of a Court Cupboard on page 26). The legs and arms of chairs and stools were now turned on the lathe as a general rule. Three other important features of the new period are the appearance on the scene of fixed upholstery, the decline in the importance attached to carving, and the widespread use of plain panelling. These three developments hang together. Needlework and embroidery at this time were extremely fine. Large sums were spent by the well-to-do on costly embroidered covers and hangings: so much so that in chairs or four-poster bedsteads the wood-work was regarded as of secondary importance, while the vogue of plain panels framed in mouldings decreased the use and the importance of carving. It is worthy of note that Charles I, who knighted Rubens and Van Dyck and employed as his Surveyor of Works the famous designer Inigo Jones, gave considerable patronage to the fine arts and is said to have been a connoisseur of furniture.

Jacobean panelling is very attractive. The furniture-makers of this era were masters in the art of spacing their panels and framing them in artistic mouldings. It is evident that a pronounced taste for applied decoration swept the country, as shown not only in the extensive use of mouldings but also in the addition of bosses of various shapes (ovals or diamonds, for example) and of pendants suggesting the split half of a cannon, fixed to the face of the wood. Jacobean designers were extremely fond of dividing the surfaces of chests or cupboards into a number of small compartments, giving the effect of a series of panels separated by the shaped mouldings and ornamented with applied bosses. The introduction of drawers became general at this time, and the typical use of divided panelling and applied decoration is illustrated in the oak chest-with-drawers shown on page 28.

[*By courtesy of "Country Life."*

MID-17TH CENTURY CHEST WITH DRAWERS

The ordinary coffer type of chest follows the same general line of development. The Jacobean chest, as distinct from the Elizabethan is not so heavy and is often plainly panelled, while any carving on it is not normally so deep. Indeed the carving is sometimes no more than the tracing of a geometrical design by the scooping of channels in the wood. These chests are obtainable, attractive and useful.

Inlaid work shows no marked advance on the Elizabethan. The use of small pieces of mother-of-pearl, ivory and ebony became popular; but this type of decoration succumbed to the Puritan influence in the middle of the century, and marquetry had to wait until the Restoration for its first period of return to fashion.

It is important to note that by the time of Charles I chairs, small stools and a number of handy and easily-moved articles had come into fairly common use, and that farmstead furniture, noticeably the dresser, was made in quantity in country districts. It is true that a mass of the finer furniture was destroyed during the Civil War and its aftermath of Puritan rule, and a further loss of important pieces occurred later in the great fire of London; but of ordinary domestic furniture the large bulk survived these events. The importation of tea and coffee, confined of course to wealthy circles, increased the demand for small tables. 'Joyn'd' stools were ubiquitous; and small Jacobean tables can be found which have one leaf—an early form which developed at about the middle of the century into the famous 'gate-legged' table. The 'joyn'd' stool differed from the Elizabethan model only in the style of its legs, which normally were turned on the lathe instead of being carved.

The gate-legged table continued to be made for at least the next one hundred years. At this stage the legs were turned very simply in the style familiar in modern copies, and though most of these tables are made of oak, specimens in elm are not unknown. The ones that command the

JACOBEAN ARM-CHAIR OF CARVED OAK
(*First half of 17th Century*)

highest prices are abnormally large or abnormally small, but a great deal depends on their surface-condition. The attractive spiral and 'barley-sugar' turning was very rare until the Restoration and greatly enhances the value of the table. A gate-leg table with the 'Spanish' foot described later on page 37 definitely belongs to a later date, but is uncommon and much to be prized.

The settle, associated with old inns, is another article that was popular, and those of the Jacobean period display the typical framed panels. Sometimes the seat is hinged towards the back and serves as a lid to the boxed-in seat which thus can be used for storage purposes. This type is more rare and of more value.

Jacobean chairs were of two sorts, plain and upholstered. The standard type of plain-wood armchair, illustrated on page 30, follows the same general lines as the late-Elizabethan chair. Its main point of difference is that its legs and arm-supports are usually turned, as shown in the photograph. Other points which distinguish the later models are the tendency of the Jacobean craftsman to divide the panelling in the back into sections and to place the scrolled cresting on the top of the back, as seen in the photograph, instead of between the uprights. In the more ambitious specimens the panelled back carries schemes of carving or inlay, but the Jacobean love of plain or sparsely decorated panels separated by mouldings is noticeable in the less ambitious chairs, and especially in settles. In single chairs, which were not yet common, the stretcher which joins the front legs is often raised some way from the ground and is sometimes broadened and carved with designs of a somewhat flat and conventional type. It is to be noted that pierced carving and the use of cane-work for the seats and back had not at this time come into fashion.

The other type, the upholstered chair, is a straight-line model which follows the same heavy lines in its framing,

YORKSHIRE AND DERBYSHIRE CHAIRS

but the back, seat and arms are padded and covered in thick and finely embroidered materials, and an open space is always left between the seat and the bottom of the upright back.

A special variety of Jacobean chair, which is very well known, was a local model. It continued to be made in certain counties long after Jacobean days, with the result that it is extremely difficult to date these chairs with any precision. They are associated particularly with Yorkshire and Derbyshire, and are an exception to the normal type of the plain-wood single chair of the period. Their legs are of ordinary turned work, and they have solid seats which are slightly recessed to take a loose cushion; but their backs are open—that is to say, the open space between the back uprights is spanned only by two carved rails of a shape which suggests the arches of arcades. The design of typical 'Yorkshire' and 'Derbyshire' chairs is shown in the photograph on page 32.

Gate-legged tables, chairs and stools, chests, settles, dressers and court-cupboards are the articles of Jacobean furniture which the collector of oak is most likely to meet.

CROMWELLIAN

In the ten years or so of the Commonwealth régime (1649 to 1660), which followed after the Civil War, gay decoration was looked on askance; furniture was extremely plain, and the chair that is generally labelled 'Cromwellian' may well have been a Puritan model. Its square underframing and turned legs are of typical Jacobean style, but its other features are very distinctive. In most cases its padded back is extremely low, with an open space between it and the seat, making the total height of the back no more than twelve inches or so, and the covering used for the back and seat is a stout leather or a simple brocade, fixed with long rows of brass-headed nails. It cannot be said quite positively that this chair belonged to the Cromwell era, for chairs having these stunted backs were made in the time of Charles I, but specimens covered in simple leather are almost certainly Puritan chairs which were made during these ten years. Spiral turning of the legs and stretchers is not inconsistent with this date, though far more rare than the plain 'knob' turning and consequently of greater value.

There is no other model except this chair that is ascribed to these particular years. The settles, dressers, tables and stools which were made widely in country districts were already of such a plain design that a restraining influence on decoration would hardly have had an effect on them, except in the case of upholstered stools where embroidery may have been deemed too 'gay' and sober leather substituted.

RESTORATION

There was a striking change in furnishing-fashions when Charles II came to the throne, but it is difficult to say which of many influences contributed most to this result. First, perhaps, came the wave of reaction against the drabness of the Puritan mode. The 'Merry Monarch' atmosphere was now paramount. Restoration dress and Restoration drama expressed the extravagant mood of the day. In the particular sphere of furniture there were other factors making for change. One was the fact that the Royalist refugees had picked up a taste for continental fashions in their years of exile across the Channel. Another was that the walnut trees planted in the reign of Elizabeth were now reaching the age of matured timber, while walnut had long been popular abroad and its importation was quite easy. A third factor was that King Charles's queen was a sister of the King of Portugal and brought as a dowry the possession of Bombay, a market-centre for trade with the East. The

35 CHARLES II ARM-CHAIR OF CARVED WALNUT

collection of oriental china, ivories and similar treasures opened up new ideas of design.

The spiral twist, which came from Portugal and had not been common hitherto, now became the general vogue for chairs, tables and cabinet-stands. A new form of scrolled leg, derived from France, also started to come into fashion. With the wide-spread use of walnut-wood carved decoration was easier to handle. Marquetry was revived in a new style; and caning was now the normal form for the seats and backs of chairs and settees.

If these influences and developments are kept in mind the fashionable furniture of Charles II's reign is not difficult to identify. The vogue of walnut is important. On the Continent walnut had been used extensively at a much earlier date, but in this country its use had been rare. It is true that oak continued to be used for chairs, large cupboards and most country-made furniture, and the date of this oak can only be determined by reference to its decoration; but after the date of the Restoration walnut was used for the fashionable furniture. The chairs and day-beds were of solid walnut, and the large pieces such as cabinets were veneered with a facing of the fashionable wood. The significant marks of the Charles II chair can be studied in the photograph on page 35. The wood of this chair is walnut throughout. It has a higher back than the Jacobean chair. The legs and arms show the spiral turning so much in favour in this period. Within the two uprights the back consists of a broad carved frame and the panel within is filled by cane-work. Caning is also employed for the seat, for loose cushions were in common use. The point to notice about the carving is that it is not solid, but pierced, and this was usual in the finer models.*

Later in the reign of Charles II this design was modified

*Note.—A flat front-stretcher of this type would be more usual than the spiral shown in the photograph.

by a new fashion. The main features remained the same, but the arm-supports and the front legs took shapes composed of curved scrolls. Instead of consisting of Jacobean or of spiral turning they were shaped in scrolls of contrasting curves suggestive of an elongated 'S', or sometimes an 'S' combined with a 'C'. Legs of this type can be seen on the rather later chairs in the photograph on page 38. They are based on the so-called 'Flemish curve', a shape derived from Spanish influence on continental decoration, and they constitute an important development, for legs of this type form a prominent feature in the furniture of the next two reigns until they were finally superseded by the cabriole leg of 'Queen Anne' fame. In arm-chairs of this date (about 1685) the outward splay of the arms is also typical.

Another feature introduced at this time is the foot known as the 'Spanish foot'. This is a curl-over shape of foot which turns outward at the base of the leg much in the fashion of a slender paw set corner-wise on each front leg. It is not the same as the round whorl foot which was characteristic of French design. This 'Spanish' foot is seen in the photograph of a William and Mary chair on page 43, and is useful in establishing the approximate date of chairs, settees and small tables.

The stools and the day-beds of this period followed the styles of the fashionable chairs. Their stretchers consisted either of spiral twists or of pierced carving of the type that was used in the cresting-rails and the front-stretchers of the chairs described. Stools, still the usual seats for meals, had two stretchers, one on each side. The day-beds sometimes had only one, and those having two are the more valuable. In the carving a favourite item of decoration is a crown supported by cherubim.

A chair which shows a striking change from the typical Charles II model is often described as 'James II' (1685 to 1688). Actually, it was probably introduced in the last

LATE RESTORATION WALNUT CHAIRS

38

five years of Charles II's reign. Its framing below the seat-level follows the same general lines as before, with a carved front stretcher set rather high up and front legs of the new scrolled shape, but its back is altogether distinctive. The back is abnormally high and narrow, and the cresting-rail of carved scroll-work curves upwards so that the top of the chair takes almost a hooped form (see the photograph on page 38). This pierced scroll carving is very different from the floral designs in the cresting of the chair on page 35, a form of design which was now discarded. The front stretcher is in the same style (or it may consist of turned work, as shown in the chair on the right of the photograph), and the stretcher itself may be slightly set back, joining the side rails instead of the front legs. Cane-work is normally used for the seat and for the long panel in the narrow back, but sometimes one or both are upholstered, and in other cases the seat is upholstered and the back consists wholly of pierced carving. The disadvantage of these light high chairs lies in the frailty of their construction, which is increased by the definite backward rake given to the back from the seat upwards. The front legs of the single chairs are simply bored into the seat above them instead of the seat-frame being tenoned between them.

The last ten years before William and Mary also witnessed a revival of inlay. The somewhat elementary work in stained woods, bone and mother-of-pearl which had characterised Jacobean inlay, first developed into gaily coloured floral designs and then began to give place to marquetry in contrasted browns or golden-yellows on a dark background. In Restoration days the latter style was probably the work of Dutch craftsmen. Marquetry was in great demand, and this was the start of a notable revival which reached a peak of skill and artistry in the subsequent reign of William and Mary. 'Grandfather' clocks were introduced at this time, and the development of the new style can be seen by comparing the earlier clocks, where the floral or geometrical inlay is reserved in small panels, with the 'all-over' fashion of the Dutch Period where intricate marquetry covers the whole long case, as seen in the photograph on page 140.

Restoration design in heavier furniture followed the Jacobean patterns; but important pieces, instead of being made of oak throughout, were veneered with walnut on oak or pear-wood, and relied for decoration on the beautiful figure obtained by cross-cutting the walnut-wood. Cabinets with glass fronts undoubtedly began to be made at this time, for Chinese and Japanese porcelain and ivories were now the fashion in wealthy houses as a result of the brisk trade with the East; but these early cabinets are very rare.

There are also the lacquer cabinets on stands. In those of the Restoration period the lacquer is usually oriental work and only the stand is English-made. The making of lacquer in this country in imitation of the oriental was only just starting a popular vogue that reached its peak in the next thirty years. The stands of the cabinets are made of soft-wood, gilded over and most elaborately and boldly carved in a continental type of design in which heavy scrolled legs play a large part. The earlier date of these rare pieces as compared with those of the next Period has to be judged by the leg-shaping. It is possible that some of the finer stands in which the intricate carving of flowers and foliage is outstanding in its delicate skill, came from the hands of Grinling Gibbons, whose work of this type is noted later (Chapter 6).

Gambling at cards was exceedingly popular, but card-tables, as such, had not yet been developed. Small oblong occasional tables, with a single drawer, were fairly common, the finer ones having spiral legs and tops veneered with figured walnut. Probably the player of ombre or faro used either these or the gate-leg table.

There existed, of course, a large class of people who did not approve of the new modes and remained faithful to the plainer models of earlier days. Walnut was the wood of fashion, but the bulk of the furniture, taken as a whole, was still made of oak, particularly in the country districts, and chestnut also was frequently used. This simple oak furniture may, therefore, be difficult to date with any accuracy; but in the case of fashionable furniture the Restoration style is easy to recognise. There are, however, many cases such as high-backed chairs, small tables or cabinet-stands, where the *late* Restoration model persisted into the early years of the William and Mary period before the new Dutch influence on design made itself generally evident.

CHAPTER 5

The Period of Dutch Influence

WILLIAM AND MARY AND QUEEN ANNE

THESE reigns saw the evolution of a great change in the design of furniture which culminated in the distinctive style generally recognised as 'Queen Anne'. It is the period *par excellence* of walnut veneer (usually on pine-wood) and of the introduction of the curved line; while, in the field of inlaid-work, English marquetry reached its high-water mark of technical skill. A large contribution to these results was made by the trend of public events. The great advance in technical skill can be attributed in no small measure to the influx of Huguenot craftsmen at the beginning of the reign of James II, while the break-away from the straight-line design was due to the impact of Dutch ideas when William and Mary came to the throne.

To most people the Queen Anne style is represented by certain features that are seen most clearly in chairs and settees. The chair shown on page 51 is chosen to illustrate these points and may be said to be 'typical Queen Anne' style. The significant features are the hooped back with its solid splat, the curved shaping of the seat-frame, and, above all, the so-called 'cabriole' leg with its clean curve from knee to foot. The cabriole leg is particularly important because it persisted in fashion, in modified forms, during a large part of the succeeding period of Georgian furniture. The word 'cabriole' refers by derivation to the bending of the knee for a forward jump. In origin this shape of leg was oriental; by adoption it was Dutch; in perfection it was

[*By courtesy of "Country Life."*

43 WILLIAM AND MARY CHAIR

English. In its perfected form it is a clean curve ending at the toe in a simple club or pad foot, or else in the well known 'claw and ball' seen in the photograph, and it is decorated on the knee only. The whole leg was cut from solid wood. The insistence on curves as illustrated by the typical chair with its cabriole leg, its hooped back, its shaped splat and its rounded seat constitutes the most striking feature of the fully developed Queen Anne style; and the process of development possesses a very particular interest.

The perfected Queen Anne style is distinctive; but the adaptation by English craftsmen of Dutch ideas in design was a gradual process, and to those collectors of old furniture who like to be able to date pieces with as much precision as can be attained, the furniture of the preceding reign (1689 to 1702) presents certain intriguing questions. The reason for the difficulty is simple enough. The furniture of William and Mary's reign represents a transitional phase in which French, Italian, Spanish, Portuguese and Dutch influences were all at work: it links the 'late-Stuart' style with 'Queen Anne': it stands between design that is predominantly of the straight-line type and is inclined to be florid and design that is predominantly curved and plain. Naturally, at each end of the reign there are border-line cases to puzzle the collector who wishes to be able to label pieces as definitely 'William and Mary'. An early William and Mary chair may bear exceedingly close resemblance to a tall high-backed James II chair, and again, at the other end of the reign, a certain type of William and Mary cabinet may be so like an early Queen Anne cabinet that it is very difficult to say for certain to which of the two reigns each belongs. This is a problem which has to be faced.

In distinguishing William and Mary furniture from late-Restoration furniture there is at least one feature which helps in the task of identification, and this feature is the 'tied' stretcher. At the beginning of the reign chairs were still being made, of course, in the characteristic late-Stuart design; but if the stretcher joining the two front legs has been discarded in favour of a 'tied' stretcher, it is fairly certain that the chair is later and belongs to the William and Mary era. The tied stretcher, which can be seen in the chair (*circa* 1690) illustrated on page 43, is the form in which flat or moulded stretchers run diagonally from the four legs to meet at the centre-point of the chair. They run in a curve, and are often crowned at the point where they meet by a small ornamental knob. This form was a continental fashion which is found occasionally in earlier models,—as early in fact as Charles II—but it became so general after 1688 that it is widely regarded as good evidence in favour of William and Mary design. It was the basic design of the stretcher-work in chairs, stools, tables and other furniture until later, during the reign of Queen Anne, the cabriole leg became the general fashion and stretchers were the exception.

In the chair shown the vase-shaped bulb on the front legs should also be noted. The 'Portuguese' bulb in its more common form of a plain ball or bun is a feature of William and Mary chair design. Incidentally, too, the coverings used at this time were characteristic. The weaving of silks and rich velvets was flourishing at Spitalfields, thanks largely to immigrant workers, and ladies of fashion vied with one another in producing very fine needle-work. As a consequence, the seats and backs of the richer type of chair and settee were often upholstered in patterned velvets and most elaborate needle-work covers. The usual style of needle-work is the slanting stitch known as *petit point.* Specimens of the 'Genoese' velvets and of chairs in the style of Daniel Marot, a designer of Franco-Dutch descent who was employed by William III, can be seen in the rooms of Hampton Court Palace.

At the other end of the reign the difficulty of distinguishing

WILLIAM AND MARY SECRETAIRE

William and Mary from Queen Anne models occurs chiefly in the case of large pieces with straight-line tops, such as cabinets and 'tall-boys'. It might be thought, possibly, that the point would be settled by the particular style of the marquetry-work. In the twenty-five years of the two reigns English marquetry reached its zenith. It was commonly used, in expensive furniture, for the decoration of the fronts of cabinets and similar models, the tops of tables and grandfather clocks. The inlay typical of the Restoration had been 'reserved' or separated in small panels, and the change which took place as the art developed was to cover most of the available surface with intricate floral and scroll patterns which culminated in the fine and delicate type known as 'sea-weed'. The marquetry of the period varies between two styles, in one of which the contrast between the woods is sharp in colour, while the other relies on the quiet contrast between darker and lighter shades of brown or golden yellows. It is true that as a general rule the more subdued and the more delicate the marquetry becomes, the later is its date, and that in the reign of Queen Anne the tendency in furniture generally was towards more sober decoration; but to date a piece by reference to changes which occurred in the style of the marquetry during the course of the two reigns is very difficult. It is not safe, for example, to infer that a particular style of marquetry was the fashion in the year 1710 because it occurs on the case of a grandfather-clock of that date; for the date of the clock is known by the date of its works, but the makers of clock-*cases* were very conservative in adhering to old styles in decoration. It may be added that English marquetry at its best was more quiet in tone than the contemporary Dutch work: the colours are better harmonised and the designs are better spaced.

This difficulty of dating straight-topped pieces, such as cabinets and chests-of-drawers, as between 'William and

Mary' and 'Queen Anne' is of so much interest to some collectors of walnut furniture that it may be worth illustrating it by an example. The photograph on page 46 shows a William and Mary Secretaire—the writing desk of the period. Not all the cabinets of the two reigns were elaborately decorated with marquetry-work: many relied, as this one does, on the beautiful golden-brown walnut veneer, so cut and matched as to make the most of the figure of the wood. The marquetry in this particular piece is confined to narrow herring-bone bands that frame the large front panel above and all the drawers below and within. (The edging of drawers with bands of veneer, showing either diagonal grain or plain cross grain or the herringbone pattern, was usual at this time.) The panel 'lets down' on iron rods to form a writing desk, and behind it are no less than fifteen drawers, all similarly veneered in figured walnut, a small cupboard, pigeon-holes and a number of concealed hiding-places. The long narrow section below the cornice, with its ovolo front, is also a drawer.

The conclusion that this secretaire is 'William and Mary' could not be drawn from its quiet tone, which might fairly be said to be in the Queen Anne manner; nor could it be drawn from the handles and lock-plates; nor from the ovolo frieze with its drawer; nor, again, from the feet. The feet at this time might be either the rounded 'bun' feet that were used generally to support heavy pieces in the later Stuart period, or the bracket feet (as shown) which were just coming into fashion in the William and Mary reign and are often replacements of the original 'bun' feet. It might be argued that the significant feature is the shape of the secretaire's straight-line cornice, for by the time of Queen Anne the curved line had taken so firm a hold on design that the normal form of Queen Anne cabinet has a curved cornice of the hooded shape. But this criterion also fails, because

49 QUEEN ANNE WALNUT BUREAU-CABINET

the straight-line or 'classical' cornice was retained in some early Queen Anne cabinets and always in chests-of-drawers and tall-boys. The fact seems to be established, however, that cabinets of this secretaire type were made in the reign of William and Mary but were not made in the subsequent reign. They were superseded in Queen Anne's reign by the cabinet-bureau of the normal form in which the lower part is a bureau with drawers and the now familiar slanting top, and the upper part is a cabinet with the usual doors and a domed cornice. A typical Queen Anne bureau-cabinet (except that the handles are somewhat later) is shown in the photograph on page 49, which illustrates the hooded top. A fine specimen of this kind may well, in spite of its sober adornment, be a 'museum piece' of great value.

The secretaire, then, is 'William and Mary' in spite of its absence of marquetry work (except for the inconspicuous bands) and its quiet and sober appearance in general; but certain other models with straight-line tops which were certainly made in the reign of Queen Anne as well as in William and Mary days are the pieces which it is difficult to assign definitely to one or other of the two reigns. These are the double chest-of-drawers or 'tall boy' and the very attractive cabinet-on-stand, which were made with a straight-line cornice in both reigns. With the cabinet-on-stand the difficulty may be smaller in so far as the stand itself gives a clue; but unless it possesses plain cabriole legs, which definitely indicate Queen Anne design, its date will still be a matter of judgment which has to rely on details of design. A typical stand may have any one of three styles: spiral legs joined by a flat stretcher, or legs of moulded or square-cut scrolls following the very late Stuart pattern, or legs of the baluster type crowned at their tops by the Portuguese bulb and tapering downwards towards the feet. None of these three forms went entirely out of fashion until

51 QUEEN ANNE CHAIR IN CARVED AND VENEERED WALNUT

the cabriole leg superseded them all. A change in the form of the Portuguese bulb is sometimes stated to be conclusive as a mark of William and Mary design. It changed its form from a simple ball to that of an inverted cup, and the latter is certainly a typical feature of William and Mary design in legs; but it lasted into Queen Anne's reign. In fine, in the case of these straight-topped pieces the collector must often be content with the knowledge that their date lies within the twenty years from 1690 to 1710.

One detail to be noted in passing concerns the pattern of veneer called 'oyster-shell', which is used in bands on important pieces. It is built up of sections of small boughs, carefully matched and set in a row. Sometimes walnut and sometimes laburnum was used to produce this special effect. The oyster pattern is prized as a token of quality. Olive wood was used in a similar way to form the background for designs in marquetry.

With the opening years of the 18th century the difficulty of dating begins to disappear as the Queen Anne style becomes fully developed. This perfected style is, of course, most generally associated with the hooped back and the cabriole leg as exemplified in the 'Queen Anne chair'. The typical settee has the same features, as if two arm-chairs had been joined into one. But chairs and settees form only one department of a style which governed a range of furniture which by this time had become wide; for a striking feature of this homely period was the large increase in the variety of articles that were now produced for domestic comfort. The design of the writing-bureau of the time, with its drawers below and its sloping front, has remained popular to this day. The winged chair was another Queen Anne development; as also were small knee-hole writing tables, bureau-cabinets, small chests-of-drawers on legs, corner-cupboards, tea-caddies, and looking-glasses for the dressing table. Chairs and tables were introduced which were specially designed for writing purposes, and the card-table proper made its appearance. Chairs, incidentally, had now taken the place of stools as the usual seats at table for meals, and the old court cupboard and buffet were out-of-date. In all the new articles, however, the Queen Anne model is not difficult to recognise, and the salient points to be noted are three,—mahogany had not yet 'arrived' to supersede the vogue of walnut; the period was one of curved lines; and the cabriole leg was the favourite support not only for chairs, stools, tables and settees but even for the stands of light cabinets and the 'low-boy' type of chests-of-drawers. The winged 'grandfather' chair was very attractive: a photograph is given on page 54 which shows the clean-cut cabriole leg with typical shell carving on the knee. In the early 18th century the arms of these chairs, and of the upholstered settees, usually curl outwards, as shown.

The perfected form of the cabriole leg which relied for its grace on its clean-cut sweep, was a gradual development. Indeed, there are William and Mary chairs which show it in process of evolution from a leg composed of Flemish scrolls, and even when the cabriole proper appeared in that reign the line of the curve was invariably obscured by carved decoration. There is, for instance, one early form in which the carving suggests the idea of a stocking. When the plain cabriole first emerged the legs were joined by slender stretchers, but they were not needed to aid the construction and they detracted from the artistic effect, and the normal chair has no stretchers. In chairs and settees (as distinct from stools) the front legs only were in cabriole form. Chairs with four cabriole legs are a little later. The perfected form was essentially simple.

Apart from the cabriole leg the special features of the typical Queen Anne chair are the disappearance of a top-cresting in favour of the simple hooped back, the flat solid

[*By courtesy of "Country Life."*

WINGED-CHAIR IN WALNUT OF QUEEN ANNE DESIGN

splat in the open back, the 'drop-in' seat, and the curved outline of the sides and front of the seat-framing. The splat, typically of fiddle-shape form, was very often quite plain, but in finer pieces it carried a modicum of carved decoration for which the scallop shell was a favourite design. The scallop-shell was a characteristic detail on the knees of the legs and is frequently found as an item of decoration on Queen Anne models of all types. When marquetry is used to decorate the splat, it is quiet in tone and is 'reserved' in panels. If a chair is decorated in marquetry throughout it is very probably of Dutch origin. Occasionally in the later years of the reign the splat is no longer entirely solid but contains a scheme of pierced carving; and this development is specially notable as linking the chair-back of Queen Anne times with the style associated with Chippendale.

One further point concerns the foot. In the earlier stages of the cabriole leg before it reached its perfected form, the foot was frequently shaped like a hoof, but the Queen Anne model was a simple pad (as illustrated in the photograph of the winged arm-chair) until the claw-and-ball became the fashion. The idea of the claw came from the Orient. The lion's paw, accompanied by a lion's mask on the bend of the leg, was extremely rare until Georgian days and was possibly a German design.

The curve beloved of the Queen Anne craftsmen is by no means confined to the hooped back, the rounded seat, the cabriole leg and the domed shaping of the tops of bureau-cabinets. The Queen Anne mirror is characteristic. English-made mirrors dated from the founding of a mirror-glass factory under the patronage of the Duke of Buckingham in the reign of Charles II; but, whereas the frames of Stuart mirrors were always of rectilinear form, the typical mirror of Queen Anne style is rounded off at its top corners and generally has an arch-shaped head. Again, if the doors of cabinet-bureaux have sunken panels, as they often do, the

WALNUT AND GILT MIRROR (*circa* 1730)

56

panels will have these shaped tops, and mirrors in the panels follow suit. The stands of the small dressing-table mirrors invariably show some curves in their lines; and in the stands of small tables with baluster legs and flat stretchers, which were very popular at this time, there is often an 'apron' of small arches connecting the legs just below their tops. A detail of this arch design which is characteristic of 'Queen Anne' is a small pendant known as a 'cusp' which hangs, as it were, from the middle of the arc. It is a point to be noted that Queen Anne tables did not always have the cabriole leg, though it gradually ousted the baluster type.

The style of the frame of the mirror varies. One type is nearly a square, with a very broad edge of convex shape, technically called a 'bolection moulding', and sometimes finished in oyster veneer,—the only frame that has straight outlines. A second type has a wide flat outer surround, a sheet, as it were, of walnut wood cut at the edges in fretted curves, as seen in the photograph on page 56. The mirror shown is a very fine specimen of slightly later date, but is characteristic of the Queen Anne era. There are also frames in gilt gesso (layers of paint on a composition), with tops of the normal arched design. The fourth kind is the narrow-edged type of frame which would be well illustrated if the flat decorated edging were removed from the mirror in the photograph.

The liking for secret drawers was strong. In the inside part of bureaux and cabinets a multiplicity of small recesses was a feature that appealed very much to the age. In the building up of these drawers and recesses there is often an architectural feeling, exemplified in important pieces by a central recess with a small domed roof and little pilasters on each side, recalling a niche in the wall of a room. The small pilasters usually conceal two upright drawers, which are found in almost all Queen Anne and early Georgian bureaux. A minor point of some interest is that in nearly all bureau-cabinets, whether of walnut or mahogany, up to about 1750, two small slides will be found below the upper doors which were probably intended to hold candle-sticks.

The rounded mouldings which run round the drawer-fronts in this period should be noted. They are usually half-round beadings a good deal broader than the very narrow 'cock-beading' which became popular for mahogany furniture towards the middle of the century.

A curious exception to the fashion for curves should be noted in the case of the Windsor chair. The normal type, familiar to all, has a plain hooped back; but this is not so in the Queen Anne style. Exceptionally to the general rule the middle struts of the back rise above the hoop, and are crowned by a broad straight cresting-rail. These earlier 'Windsors' are comparatively rare and of more value than the ordinary shape.

Taking the Queen Anne style as a whole, it was a period of plain furniture. It is true that elaborate marquetry-work continued to be used on important pieces, and particularly on the cases of grandfather clocks; but these pieces were made for rich patrons. The elaborate design is not representative of the general demand of the well-to-do classes any more than are the lacquer cabinets on ornately carved and gilded stands, of which mention will be made below. The attraction of the normal Queen Anne furniture lies in its simplicity, the beauty of the wood and the restraint shown in its decoration. Natural beauty and a quiet taste combined in a homely and comfortable style.

Finally, there is the subject of Lacquer; for it was in the Period of Dutch Influence that English-made lacquer first made its appearance. The fashionable craze for oriental 'Lack-work', or 'Japan work', as it was called, began in the reign of Charles II, although occasional Chinese and Japanese pieces had been imported by traders at a much earlier date. By the time of William and Mary, however, its popularity had become so great that the art had been taken up in this country, probably under Dutch supervision. This was not just the use of a varnish-paint, as in the last quarter of the 18th century, but a serious attempt at a reproduction of the actual process used in the east.

The chief examples of this work are the square-built cabinets mounted on stands. The lacquer may be red, green, black or silver, and the silver lacquer is the most rare. The normal stand is English-made, elaborately carved and gilded over. An approximate date can be assigned to a stand by a detailed study of its design, but the cabinet itself is another story. Sometimes the lacquer work was done in Japan or China, and sometimes the lacquer is English work. The English lacquer varies in quality from the amateurish to the very fine; and the finer work is so good a copy of the oriental that expert knowledge is required to tell it. It is more rare than the oriental; and if a collector is offered a cabinet at a price which assumes that the lacquer is English-made, he would be well advised to consult a dealer who is a specialist in this difficult subject.

. . . . . .

The walnut furniture of these two reigns makes a special appeal to many collectors. This is the reason why particular mention has been made of the rather fine point of dating certain pieces as between 'William and Mary' and 'Queen Anne'. Summing up on that point, it may be said that on any type of the furniture which was made in the two reigns the perfected or clean-cut cabriole leg is a sure indication of Queen Anne. Similarly it may be accepted that the Secretaire with a falling-front is a William and Mary model, and that the bureau and the bureau-cabinet are Queen Anne models. In the case of the tall-boys and the chests or cabinets-on-stands which have straight line tops the date can only be placed as lying between 1690 and 1710 unless there is evidence, such as marquetry of the later style, which definitely points to the Queen Anne date.

For the collector of smaller pieces a promising field is opened by the large number of knee-hole writing (or dressing?) tables, and occasional or dressing tables, which were made for the smaller rooms which were fashionable in Queen Anne's day. The graceful little walnut table with either cabriole legs or legs joined by flat stretchers is both attractive and useful. Sets consisting of a table, two candle-stands and a looking-glass were very popular in this period. The candle-stands, made of walnut, were of the same height as the table.

CHAPTER 6

The Georgian Period. I

EARLY GEORGIAN (1715–1740)

Up to this time the Period styles are distinguished by the names of Kings or dynasties, and the only names of individual artists associated with the design and decoration of furniture are those of Inigo Jones, who was primarily an architect, Grinling Gibbons, the genius at carving who was first discovered by Evelyn, the diarist, and Daniel Marot, a Franco-Dutchman who received commissions from William of Orange. After Queen Anne a change takes place. Period styles begin to be named after famous designers such as Chippendale, Hepplewhite, Adam and Sheraton; but before the date when the influence of Thomas Chippendale radically changed the prevailing fashion there were twenty-five years or so of furniture which can only be classified under the general title 'Early Georgian'.

The outstanding development of these interim years was the change-over in fashionable furniture from walnut wood to mahogany, for which 1718 to 1720 may be accepted as the approximate date. It was a slow change, for the duties payable on the importation of mahogany were very severe. There was also a notable change of taste. The vogue of marquetry came to an end as walnut gradually went out of fashion, but in all other respects than in marquetry Queen Anne design had been plain and simple, and this simplicity was affected greatly by the taste which characterised the new era. In the hands of the Early Georgian designers the Queen Anne style was elaborated. This is the period

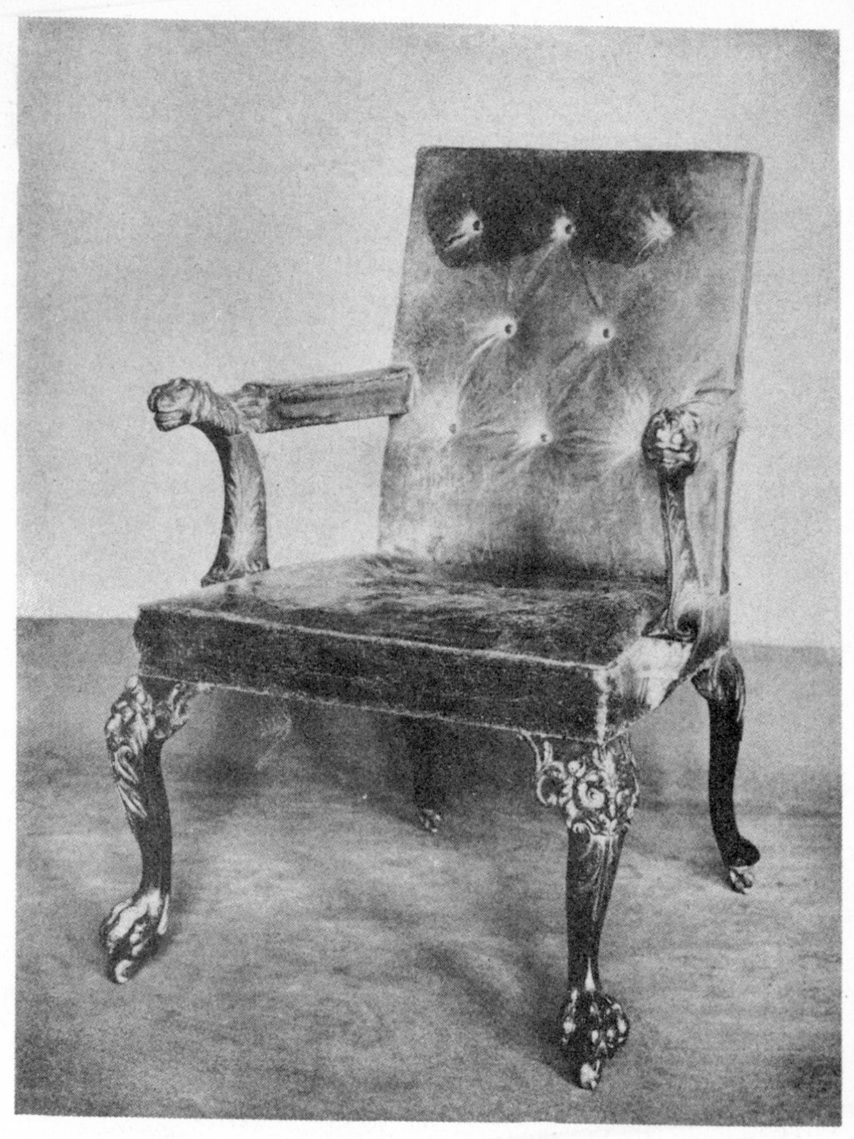

EARLY GEORGIAN MAHOGANY ARM-CHAIR WITH 'LION' DECORATION

of the type of chair associated with the name of the artist Hogarth, in which the hoop of the back is made more complex by adding a cross-rail below its top, the splat starting from this secondary rail instead of beginning at the top of the back. This was one instance of elaboration, and others affected all types of furniture. It was the era when a lion's or a satyr's mask was carved on the knee of the cabriole leg; when short and squat cabrioles were commonly used instead of bracket feet as the supports for large and heavy pieces; and when the solid splat of the Queen Anne chair was too simple for the taste of the day so far as the fashionable world was concerned. Pierced carving of the central splat, which had begun in the later years of Queen Anne, now became a definite vogue. There was, in fact, an all-round tendency towards a more pretentious style. One particular feature of this tendency may be noted in the arms of chairs and settees where the ends of the arms are curved outwards and carved in the shape of eagles' or animal heads. The pointed beak of the eagle's head was perhaps inconvenient, for this fashion did not last very long and ends rounded in a simple scroll were substituted in later designs. Besides the lion's or satyr's mask another favourite decoration for the knees of legs was the cabochon (or oval jewel) and leaf design. This detail was used by Chippendale later on, but Chippendale never used the lion's mask.

The style of this early mahogany furniture is well illustrated by the arms and thick cabriole legs of the upholstered chair shown on page 62 which displays the lion's mask and paw decoration at its best.

The general features of Queen Anne design still governed the outline of furniture as a whole, and walnut was used side by side with mahogany at least in the case of chairs and settees, but the taste of the time was expressed both in ornate decoration—the 'decorated Queen Anne' style—and also in a definite heaviness of touch. In wall-furniture, such as side-tables and cabinets, the influence of architecture was very marked. The architects who followed the tradition of Inigo Jones and Christopher Wren were wedded to the classic 'orders', and the decorations designed by them for the Queen Anne and Early Georgian houses were undoubtedly fine and dignified work, but their treatment of door-frames, mantel-pieces and walls, though admirable as to line and proportion, was imbued with a certain 'classic' formality which encouraged a heavy and grand tone in the furniture which went with them. One of these architects was William Kent, who returned in the year 1719 from an educational sojourn in Rome and achieved a great name in artistic circles. Some of his work is deservedly famous (the Horse Guards building, for example), but features such as the Ionic capital or the Doric column may be 'right' in an architectural scheme but result in a ponderous and laboured effect when embodied in a piece of domestic furniture; and the keynote of Kent's designs in furniture is a combination of grandiose detail with a heaviness of composition which is typical of this era. Heavy scrolls of foliage, eagles and lions play a large part in these designs. Accordingly many Early Georgian models carry strong identification-marks in their combination of Queen Anne line with a rather pronounced architectural treatment. A bureau-bookcase, for example, will combine 'classic' architectural features with mirrors of typical Queen Anne shape in the panels of its mahogany doors. One very usual architectural feature on Early Georgian cabinets is the 'broken' pediment. Wall-furniture inclined to be monumental.

Lacquer was favoured for grandfather clocks (mahogany clock-cases seem to be later), and gilding, as might be expected, was popular. Some walnut chairs are decorated in gold, and chairs intended to be specially impressive were occasionally covered entirely in gilt. Among wealthy people there was a rage for side-tables with heavy marble or imitation marble tops which have massively carved underframings and adaptations of the cabriole leg that are very ornate and gilded all over.

Even in the case of the 'grandfather' chairs, where the upholstery is the main feature, the Early Georgian examples are less attractive than the Queen Anne models of the type shown on page 54. The short cabriole legs tend to be more clumsy or rather ornate.

On the whole the marks of this transitional phase between the Queen Anne style and the Chippendale style are well defined and easy to recognise. So far as the furniture is made of mahogany it cannot be confused with 'Queen Anne'; but it is very difficult to draw the line between some of the chairs, settees and dining-tables made in these years and certain early Chippendale models. Queen Anne shaping was still the fashion for chairs and settees when Chippendale was starting his career as a designer; and he followed this shaping in his early models before he developed his own style. Again, in the case of dining-tables, the early Georgian model with cabriole legs and hinged flaps remained the pattern in early Chippendale days. In this matter, however, Mr. Herbert Cescinsky, an eminent authority on 18th century furniture, called attention to the point that the mahogany normally used by Chippendale was not the same variety of wood. The mahogany of the earlier date was a hard straight-grained Cuban variety with very little figure and a golden colour.

. . . . . .

It is said that the appointment of Master Carver to King George I was held by the famous Grinling Gibbons. The work of Gibbons belongs to the field of architecture rather than to that of domestic furniture, but no one who is interested in artistic craftsmanship can afford to ignore this brilliant artist who influenced the style of interior decoration from the reign of Charles II onwards up to the time of his death in 1720.

Some uncertainty has been expressed as to whether his name was Gibbons or Gibbon, but there can be little doubt that it was Gibbons, and there is no doubt at all about the quality of his art. He was introduced by Evelyn to Charles II in the year 1671, and his unique gifts as a carver were recognised by his wealthy patrons and led to a long association with the still more famous Sir Christopher Wren. Though he was also a sculptor and a first-rate exponent of the fine plasterwork done at this time, he is best known for his extraordinary carving in lime and other soft woods. His festoons of flowers, fruits and foliage are carved with a delicacy and a natural touch that probably never have been surpassed. His work can be seen in St. Paul's Cathedral, and there are famous examples at Oxford and Cambridge. There was, of course, a host of followers who imitated the Grinling Gibbons manner with varying degrees of success, but no one who has seen his authentic work would have much difficulty in distinguishing the hand of this unique master of carved decoration.

CHAPTER 7

The Georgian Period. II

THOMAS CHIPPENDALE (1740–1779)

Of the individual designers and craftsmen who brought renown to English furniture the first and the greatest was Thomas Chippendale, and a standard book on 18th century furniture usually devotes a large proportion of space to the work of this master. The modern tendency to 'de-bunk' famous names has not spared Chippendale, but there is no great point in raising the question whether he was actually the author of all the designs in his published book, or in proving that there were contemporary designers and contemporary craftsmen whose work reached a very high standard of excellence but whose names have remained relatively obscure. It is true that the designers and the engravers of the plates in the 'catalogues' published in this period served first one master and then another, and the difficulty inherent in distinguishing the work of a particular designer or cabinet-maker is frankly admitted by all experts. Nevertheless it is quite clear that Chippendale was a creative artist who stamped his mark on the fashions of a period which is widely regarded as the greatest era in the history of British cabinet-making.

The precise date when Chippendale set up workshops in London is not certain; but it seems safe to say that by the year 1745 he was starting to make a name for himself as a result of his personal taste and skill. For a proper appreciation of his work it is necessary to remember that he lived at a time when the fashionable world held a lofty position that was singularly remote from 'the vulgar crowd' and spent a great deal of its ample leisure in playing daintily with the luxuries of life. The latest whim of fashion was enormously important, and vogues in furniture, as in everything else, were subject to sudden shifts of fancy. The designer who was also a business-man had to pay some attention to these vagaries, although he might hope, as an artist, to mould them. It is confusing, therefore, for those who are seeking for a defined picture of the Chippendale style to find that it went through various phases. The first question is what is meant by the term when a chair or a table, a cabinet or a mirror, is given the title 'Chippendale'.

To label a chair 'Chippendale' might have been any one of three meanings. It might mean (*a*) that it was designed by Chippendale and actually made in Chippendale's workshops; or (*b*) that it might reasonably be *presumed* to be so, because it is made in Chippendale's style and also displays super-excellent craftsmanship; or (*c*) simply that it is a contemporary piece made in the recognised Chippendale style. The first of these meanings could only be proved by producing the original documents of sale, and few pieces exist which are so identified. The second is a matter of connoisseur judgment, and the best experts are never dogmatic on such an extremely difficult question, but the verdict of an accepted expert that a particular piece is 'presumptive Chippendale' would give it, of course, a very high value. Pieces of these two classes, however, are probably outside the reach of the collector unless his purse is unusually large. The third sense of the label 'Chippendale' is the one in which it is generally used. It is a recognised fact that the firm of Chippendale could not have produced a one-hundredth part of the volume of furniture attributed to them. 'Chippendale', in current usage, can only mean 'in the Chippendale style'. In point of fact, most of the carved mahogany that belongs to the period of forty years between 1740 and 1780 is apt loosely to be called 'Chippendale' unless there are details of line or decoration that bring it within the popular idea of Hepplewhite or Adam design. It is possible to do much better than that. In 'placing' the carved mahogany furniture of this middle section of the 18th century the first task amounts to this—to be able to recognise the characteristics that justify one of the four main labels, Early Georgian, Chippendale, Adam and Hepplewhite. If the *typical* styles are clearly conceived, a hybrid piece can be named as such and labelled in terms of its approximate date.

The particulars about Chippendale which are now generally accepted as facts are as follows. He was baptised in 1718 and was brought to London from Yorkshire, at a date unknown, by his father who was himself a craftsman. In 1749 he had a shop in Long Acre, and 1753 he had larger premises situated in St. Martin's Lane. He published the first edition of his book *The Gentleman and Cabinet-Maker's Director* in 1754, the second edition in 1755 (not 1759) and the third in 1762. In 1760 he was elected a member of the Society of Arts where his fellow-members included famous people such as Reynolds, Garrick and Horace Walpole who were prominent in artistic circles. His first partnership (with a Mr. Rannie) terminated in 1766. He took his book-keeper, Thomas Haig, into partnership in 1771, and he died in the year 1779. The business was carried on by his son in a partnership known as Haig and Chippendale.

There were three hundred subscribers to his book the *Director* in the year 1754, including craftsmen, artists, members of many professions and people of very high social position, and it is a reasonable assumption that by the year 1750 he was widely regarded as a man of mark whose taste was a force in current design; but a reputation of this kind is not built up in a few short years, and it seems to be a further reasonable assumption that Chippendale

A 'TYPICAL' STRAIGHT-LEGGED CHAIR

70

was well set up in business at least as early as 1740 and was making his mark between 1745 and 1750. It is clear that the great period of his influence lay between 1754 and 1770.

The years 1740 to 1750 introduce the first of the four phases which are usually distinguished in the Chippendale style. Chippendale during these pre-*Director* years was doubtless using his personal taste and his profound knowledge of craftsmanship in modifying the Early Georgian style which he found in the furniture then in fashion. Its characteristics in the way of heaviness have been sketched briefly in the last chapter, and Chippendale's bent was towards lightness. In the case of chairs the marks of Chippendale's new influence are the further modification of the hooping of the back in the direction of a straight-line cresting, the further lightening of the central splat, and the lessening of the general effect of heaviness which characterised Early Georgian handling of the basic design of the Queen Anne style. The cabriole leg still held the field, and the wood used was sometimes walnut, but by the time that Chippendale was influencing fashion the heavy duty on mahogany had been mitigated, while the hooped back of Queen Anne design was fast becoming a thing of the past, replaced by an almost straight-line top which in its most attractive shape suggests the idea of a cupid's bow. To many people the Chippendale style used to be associated almost exclusively with this type of chair with cabriole legs and claw-and-ball feet; and in the hands of Chippendale they were very attractive, combining graceful lines with an impression of strength—a combination which, indeed, was a feature of all his best work. The corner-chair, having a semi-circular back containing two splats and a single cabriole leg in front, was also introduced at this time, but is not illustrated in the *Director*.

This early manner was only a first phase; and so far as it embodied Queen Anne features (notably the cabriole leg) it was not the 'typical' Chippendale chair which finally emerged. His 'typical' chair may fairly be said to be represented by the model shown on page 70 which was actually designed by Thomas Chippendale (the seat is upholstered in modern velvet). But this design, which naturally varies in its detailed drawing, was only gradually evolved. Chippendale as a business-man had competitors in other designers such as Ince and Mayhew and Robert Manwaring, who were well enough known to publish books of designs. The latest whim of the fashionable world was a thing that he could not afford to ignore; but this is where he exploited his talents. The genius of the man lay in using his taste, combined with consummate craftsmanship, in adapting the shifting trends of fashion. It is correct to speak of two phases of his work as his Gothic phase and his Chinese phase, but it is a mistake to think of either of these as his exclusive style at any stage or as representing his typical manner. Their importance lies in the style which emerged as a result of his handling of these fashions. Both are of doubtful artistic merit, but the collector has to know something about them.

A book on 'Gothick' designs by one, Batty Langley, was published in 1747. Edwards and Darly published a book called *Chinese Designs* in 1754. In the latter year designs in both of these styles appeared in Chippendale's book, the *Director*. The Gothic craze may perhaps be attributed to Batty Langley and Horace Walpole. The new outbreak of 'Chinese taste', following on the vogue of lacquer which had not yet lost its popularity, is commonly attributed to Sir William Chambers whose pagoda-like structures in Kew Gardens are well known; but although Chambers undoubtedly was a great influence in 'pushing' this cult of oriental design, to maintain that he introduced the fashion is demonstrably incorrect. That point, however, is not important except as a matter of historical accuracy. As

CHIPPENDALE 'LADDER-BACK' CHAIR

regards the Chippendale designs which these fashions produced, both of the tastes, the Chinese and the Gothic, can be seen exemplified in a pure form. There are pieces of furniture, particularly chairs, which can be said to be wholly in the Gothic taste, and there are pieces, noticeably china-cases, hanging shelves and gilded mirror-frames, which are more or less wholly in the Chinese taste. In 'Gothick' chairs the design of the back suggests the tracery of a Gothic window. They are exercises in the Pseudo-Gothic whose artistic merit is open to question. The Chinese designs are distinguished mainly by open frets and lattice-work, by pagoda-shaped tops in the case of cabinets, and in mirror-frames by pierced carving of an exotic type, a gilded complex of curves and branches in which curious Eastern birds are a feature. The china-cases are often graceful and the mirrors are often over-extravagant, but in any case both the Chinese and the Gothic are, in their pure form, acquired tastes. The interest of these special phases lies not so much in the rare models which can be said to be wholly 'in the Chinese taste' or wholly 'in the Gothic taste' as in any effect that these vogues produced on the typical Chippendale style in design.

These Chinese and Gothic influences were in line with Chippendale's own predilection for obtaining an effect of lightness. The *Director*, it is true, contains some designs that are heavy and extravagant, particularly in the case of console tables (tables designed to be fixed to the wall, with underframings of bracket form) which, like the mirrors, were made in soft-wood and intricately carved and gilded; but these are not *typical* creations at all. Chippendale's gift for picking features from the passing vogues and adapting them to his own taste is best seen in the mahogany furniture in which he developed a style of his own. His eclectic method is easy to follow in analysing his typical work. It is clear, for example, that certain features of the

French style, which at his time was the 'Louis Quinze', appealed to the designer very strongly. It is obvious, again, that he had a special weakness for the C scroll, which appears again and again in his carving. The Gothic and the Chinese tastes contributed in a similar way. The attractive features in both these vogues were seized on and adapted to suit his taste. In the 'typical' chair (see page 70) the points to be noted are the cresting-rail of a shape suggesting a cupid's-bow, the straight legs and the interlacing strap effect in the open design of the carved splat. The style, in fact, which can fairly be regarded as typical 'Chippendale' whether in chairs or in other furniture, was a composite style which he evolved himself at the time when he definitely led the fashion, and was a style culled from many sources.

Special points to be noted in the typical chair concern its height and the shape of its legs. Its height is important: a Chippendale chair normally measures from 3 feet 1 inch to 3 feet 2½ inches from the top of its back to the level of the floor. Chairs of later designers were usually lower. The straight square leg was the general shape after about the year 1750. The front legs of his earlier chairs were, of course, in the cabriole form, which Chippendale inherited from existing fashion, and indeed he never at any stage discarded the cabriole leg altogether. It is to be noted that with the straight leg the use of stretchers was revived. In the case of arm-chairs a detail to watch is the way in which the arms are finished, the eagle's head of earlier days being replaced by a scrolled end.

The range of the furniture listed in the *Director* is very extensive. Dining-tables, side-tables, library and writing tables, card-tables, small tripod tables, bureaux and bureau-bookcases, drawing-room chests of drawers (then called 'commodes'), china-cases and hanging shelves, fire-screens and candle-stands, wine-coolers and tea-caddies, organ-cases, four-poster bedsteads and wardrobes—these are only some of the models in which the collector can trace the characteristic details which go to make up the Chippendale manner. It is probable that the china-case proper (as distinct from the glass-fronted bureau-bookcase) was an original creation by Chippendale, and the same is true of the small tripod-table designed either as a tray for wine or for tea or for exhibiting the fashionable trinkets of the time. Afternoon tea became very fashionable about the year 1760. The side-tables designed by Chippendale were *not* sideboards in the modern sense.

In the case of many of these articles such as the bureau-bookcase, the chest-of-drawers, the library table or the dining-table (usually round or oval with two large flaps), the essential lines of the mid-18th century models in plain or carved mahogany are well-known, for considerable numbers have survived and they have been extensively copied in modern times. The dining-table changed its character completely in the hands of Chippendale's successors, as noted on page 117, but most of the other models did not, though they changed their appearance in many respects as plain mahogany passed out of fashion and daintiness came to be preferred to strength. The points which the collector has to note are the features which distinguish the designs of the Chippendale era from the succeeding styles, and the details which indicate superior quality among the several grades of 'Chippendale' furniture.

The distinguishing features of Chippendale mahogany, of which the greatest is the combination of grace with strength, will be clear when the characteristics of Adam, Hepplewhite and Sheraton design are studied. As regards the signs of quality, it is to be noted that there were three grades in the furniture of the time. In the middle of the 18th century there were many able designers who were engaged in following the current fashions, and many fine craftsmen were making the goods, such as Ince and Mayhew, the

Gillows, the Seddons and others of whom some particulars are given in Chapter 13. Further, craftsmen all over the country were busy copying the London designs. There were two grades of the finer furniture and there was the humbler class of country-made furniture. The finer furniture, which was normally made of Spanish mahogany, was either specially commissioned by wealthy patrons or was designed for the well-to-do classes in general. The first grade is of superfine quality and displays exceptional carved decoration. A good example would be a chair or settee with the famous 'ribbon-back' decoration, and another less ornate example would be the beautiful serpentine-fronted chest-of-drawers which is illustrated in the Frontispiece. In chairs a sign of this exceptional quality is carved shaping of the lower edge of the front and sides of the frame of the seat. The second grade is relatively plain, though the work and the finish is first-class. An example would be a fine specimen of the 'ladder back' chair, such as the one illustrated on page 73, or a fine specimen of the 'typical' chair showing finished treatment in all its details. It is this second grade and the country-made grade, which is plain but often very attractive, that the collector can reasonably hope to acquire. The task for the discerning collector is to watch for the detailed touches which characterise the Chippendale style in the hands of first-class cabinet-makers. A note of some of these details follows.

Many of the touches which indicate quality were based on the avoidance of heaviness in design. The Chinese and the Gothic vogues suggested three of Chippendale's methods —open lattice-work, open frets, and the use of applied fret decoration. The effective use of lattice work is well seen in his hanging book-shelves which are light little models with lattice sides. The open fret was especially suitable for small pieces such as urn-tables, or the table shown on

A CENTRE TABLE

page 78. This table is, of course, an exceptional piece as shown by the carving along the under-edge of its frieze, the fine carving on the knees of its legs and the exquisite grace of the whole design. Incidentally it shows how the cabriole leg was adapted for delicate drawing-room furniture. The *applied* fret was used on heavier pieces. In wardrobes or chests-of-drawers, for example, the outside angles of the front are bevelled, as seen in the photograph on page 82, and a strip of fret decoration is added. Grandfather clocks are similarly treated. Again, in the case of square legs the inner edge of each leg is usually 'chamfered' (the technical term for pared-off), the two outside faces are decorated with a fret or some other form of light carving and the outer edge shows a line of beading. Side-tables, which were rectangular and oblong, were often built with marble tops and the earlier models, as might be expected, were usually made with cabriole legs, but if the legs were square, as was normally the case after 1750, they were chamfered and treated as just described with the aim of achieving a light effect. In the best tables of this type the frieze of the frames below the tops shows a continuous band of fine fret carving which contrasts with the Adam type of 'classical' decoration as seen in the table illustrated on page 87.

Upholstered chairs with square-shaped backs remained popular throughout this period, but the shape of the legs changed with the fashion. When the cabriole leg gave way to the square, the legs were, as usual, connected with stretchers and the best models are in open frets.

The tripod form of support should be specially noted, for the finest designs undoubtedly date from Chippendale's time. A table is shown on page 80, and as these small tables were extremely popular and were made with great care and in large numbers they are specially worth the collector's attention. In Chippendale's earlier tripod-tables the feet are of the claw-and-ball design, there are two swells on the central column and the edge of the better quality table is raised in a rim of sharp carving of which the simplest form is the 'pie-crust' pattern. The table illustrated is finished in black and gold lacquer, and shows the 'pie-crust' edge and the type of carving which decorates the finer specimens. In other models the feet are more slender, there may be only one vase-shaped swell on the column and the top may be edged with a pierced gallery. In the

CHIPPENDALE TRIPOD TABLE (*circa* 1760)

humbler types the top is plain. The tripod-form was used also for lamp-stands and fire-screens (the latter usually in square-shaped frames), and in all these cases the test of quality is the delicacy and sharpness of the carved decoration on the central column, the knees and the feet. Humbler tripods have plain pad feet.

In card-tables the legs are graceful, cabriole at first and square-shaped later, and in the finer specimens, the edges of the top are carved. The most valuable shape is the serpentine, and small fret brackets between the legs and the top are further signs of superior grade. In wine-coolers the normal Chippendale type is an octagonal bucket in plain mahogany, bound with brass bands and mounted on a stand with square legs which are not tapered. Carved decoration on wine-coolers is exceptional, and if the legs are of cabriole form, the piece is rare and has a higher value.

In larger pieces in the Chippendale style quality is similarly marked by details, though the line and proportion are the main points. Thus in bureaux, which follow the Queen Anne pattern in their slanting tops with drawers below, the finer pieces are lined with oak or mahogany, the mahogany panels show good figure, and the brass handles are beautifully chased in scroll designs of French inspiration. In bureau-bookcases the point to watch is the placing and sharpness of the carved decoration. The glass-fronted book-case, with cupboards below, was always treated as an important piece by the best makers of the Chippendale school. The tracery in the windows should be well balanced and attractive in design, and the top should be crowned by carved decoration most commonly consisting of a broken pediment with a frieze below it of fretted ornament or of the type of 'classical' carved detail which the earlier Georgian architects favoured. Wardrobes, on the other hand, have plain straight tops, and the marks of quality are the shaping

CHIPPENDALE MAHOGANY TALL-BOY (*circa* 1760)

of the body (the serpentine is regarded as the best), the chamfering of the angles at each side of the front, and carved mouldings on the panels of the doors. Serpentine shaping and chamfered angles are also the marks of the best chests-of-drawers, and if the top drawer has a let-down front and is 'fitted' as a writing or a dressing-table, the piece will be one of exceptional value. A serpentine-fronted chest-of-drawers of fine quality of about 1760 is illustrated in the Frontispiece. It also shows the finely figured 'curl' mahogany which began to be employed at about 1755 for the veneering of important panels. Large writing-tables are always exceptional. Chippendale's large library tables are superb in design and construction alike, but the best of them, decorated on all four sides, are hardly within the reach of the average purse.

The double chest-of-drawers shown on page 82 has been chosen to illustrate some of these points. The special details that mark its quality are (1) the bands of fret carving, (2) the chamfered angles of the front, and (3) the carved ogee-shaped feet. The normal foot for this type of furniture (chests, bookcases, bureaux, etc.) was the straight-edged bracket type of foot shown in the photograph on page 46 of a William and Mary secretaire. The ogee foot is a typical detail in Chippendale furniture of the higher grade.

Handles and lock plates should always be noted. In all furniture which contains drawers the finish given to the handles and lock-plates is a sure indication of quality-grade, and the typical patterns are worth special study (see the Note on this subject in Chapter 13).

. . . . . .

The pre-*Director* phase based on Queen Anne, the Gothic phase and the Chinese phase have been mentioned. In speaking of the fourth of the four phases which writers distinguish in the Chippendale style, the reference is to 'the French taste'. This vogue is not very happily named since French influence on English design was not by any means a new thing. Chippendale himself in his early work had borrowed ideas from the Louis Quinze style, and throughout his career his carved decoration often shows details, such as the cabochon-and-leaf design, of French inspiration. The new demand for curves in the latest French style seems to have started early in the 1760's after the close of the Seven Years' War, and Chippendale's designs in this latest fashion, mostly chairs and settees of various kinds, have legs of a decorated cabriole form ending in feet which are typically French. The most usual foot is a round curled scroll. This phase of design, which stands clearly apart from the 'typical Chippendale' is, from one point of view, of special interest, for this new cult of the curved outline combined with a certain delicacy of build made the reputation of the Hepplewhite style as described and pictured in the following chapter.

It remains to add that in the late 1760's another new influence was shaping design, and one, indeed, of great importance. This was a revival of 'classical' teaching on new lines by the Adam brothers, a departure from current ideas of decoration which marks the close of the Chippendale tradition. When this artist-craftsman dissolved his first partnership in the middle '60's, furniture made in plain mahogany was losing its grip on the public taste. A new era in fashion was dawning and a revival of inlay was now on its way as well as the novel Adam teaching. Chippendale had used inlaid work on occasion, but had used it sparingly and with great restraint. In fact it was proved by Mr. Percy Macquoid, as quoted by Mr. Frederick Litchfield, that Chippendale made inlaid satinwood furniture very soon after the new wood became popular; but this was in his last few years. 'Typical Chippendale' came to an end, as far as the fashionable world was concerned, when plain carved mahogany lost its hold.

. . . . . .

The references to Chippendale's bent towards lightness may strike the reader as a little curious when he comes to consider the styles that followed, for fashion proceeded to grow lighter and lighter, in weight, in colour and in form, right up to the closing years of the century. The Chippendale style is a half-way house between the heavy Early Georgian design and the type of production of the Sheraton era which sacrificed strength to dainty appearance. The combination of strength with grace is the keynote of Thomas Chippendale's style. He indulged at times in extravagant models, but no piece of furniture is worthy to be classed as 'Chippendale style' unless it conveys an impression of balance that is due to a very keen eye for proportion. The touch of the artist is always present.

The great majority of Chippendale work was done in mahogany; but one has to remember that the London fashions were copied by small makers all over the country, not only for many years after the designs had ceased to be the fashion in London, but also in other woods than mahogany. Thus it is exceedingly difficult to date country-made pieces, and it is quite possible to find chairs of Chippendale design of, say, 1760 which are made in walnut.

. . . . . .

A note on the so-called 'Irish Chippendale' is given in Chapter 13.

CHAPTER 8

The Georgian Period. III

THE ADAM STYLE AND HEPPLEWHITE STYLE

BETWEEN the time when Chippendale's influence was all-pervasive and the 1790's when the Sheraton vogue was in full swing lies a period of striking change and development in which two famous names stand out—the Adam brothers and Hepplewhite.

The Adam brothers were architects and designers who transformed the current fashion in building and exercised a profound influence on all types of interior decoration. George Hepplewhite was a craftsman and designer who had none of the social position of the Adams but whose taste resulted in a style or manner which is widely regarded as specially attractive. Hepplewhite was a great admirer of some features of the Adam style and embodied them in his own designs, but he approached the art of designing furniture from a different standpoint, and typical Hepplewhite mahogany furniture is quite distinct from the Adam creations. The normal Adam style is a clear-cut conception, easy to grasp and to recognise in whatever medium it may be expressed. The Hepplewhite style, on the other hand, is a term that has been used loosely and needs definition.

THE ADAM STYLE

The Adam brothers were not themselves makers of furniture, but their influence on the design of furniture in the last four decades of the 18th century can hardly be exaggerated. Robert Adam, son of a Scottish architect,

ADAM MAHOGANY SIDE-TABLE (1772)

came to London after travelling in France and Italy, and at the age of 34 was a leading figure in his profession. He had been a pupil of the famous architect Piranesi, and during his studies he had made friends with Pergolesi, Angelica Kauffmann and other artists whose work was subsequently embodied in his schemes of decoration. In London he worked with his brother James in a partnership ever since known as 'The Adelphi'. In 1762 he was decorating Sion House for the Duke of Northumberland, and 1767 he designed Kenwood for the Earl of Mansfield. From first to last the key to his work was his great devotion to the classical 'orders' of architecture, and his avowed object, in his own words, was to transfuse 'the beautiful spirit of antiquity' through all parts of the decoration of a house. His aim was to give to classical art-forms, designed to be seen under sunny skies, a consistent setting in British homes, whether the home was in smoky London or stood in a park in the countryside. The movement expressed a growing re-action against the romantic 'rococo' style which had reigned so long at the Court of France and had had its influence on the Chippendale style. Furniture, in the limited sense, was only a part of the general scheme. The interpretation of the Adelphi designs in the actual construction of tables and so on was entrusted to eminent cabinet-makers such as Chippendale (notably at Harewood House), Hepplewhite, Seddon or Gillow.

Previous English use of the classic idea had been definitely heavy. The new vogue made a fetish of lightness, but it was not so much lightness of the furniture itself as a light air in its ornamentation and a literal lightness in its colour-scheme. The lead given by Chippendale in reaction from Early Georgian taste turned out to be only a first step. The cult of delicacy and elegance that started its career in the 1760's went a great deal further than Chippendale, and in the hands of the Adams it broke new ground. Everyone is familiar with the typical mantelpiece of Adam design with its straight, chaste outline, its slender columns, its narrow fluted bands, the little oval or round ornaments technically known as 'paterae', and the plaques of graceful classical figures. The details are dainty and sometimes exquisite, and the effect achieved is a kind of beauty that a critical eye might describe as cold. A chaste cool grace was the order of the day. Tall gilt tripod stands for lamps or vases, designed in the Roman style, were typical creations; and so also were large wall-mirrors in narrow and delicately drawn gilded frames.

The Adams were designers posssessed of a theory which might perhaps be described as totalitarian. The interior decoration of a house should be complementary to the building itself; and, if the building itself was pseudo-classical, the ceilings and the walls of the rooms, the friezes, the doors, the fire-places and the wall-lights should be all cast in the same mould. Indeed, casting in a mould in a literal sense was a large part of the method employed. The decorations of ceilings and door-frames—the Greek honeysuckle, the slim festoons and the flowery sprays of acanthus leaf—were mechanically cast in a stucco-composition and the whole was coloured in chaste tints. The work of this type was carried out largely by Italian craftsmen, and artists such as Angelica Kauffmann were engaged to fill the important spaces with paintings in appropriate style.

The effects of this theory on furniture were twofold: the beauty of plain mahogany was at a discount, and surface-decoration became the rage. First came painting, and then the veneering of surfaces in light-coloured woods set off by inlaid or painted designs. The Adam chair, to take an example, is not normally made of mahogany. Chaste outline and light colours being the watchwords of the day, the Adam chair is normally painted and has slim straight legs, and its back, padded more often than not, is of simple outline, oval or shield-shaped or round or square. In the cases where the chairs are made of mahogany the classical touch is supplied by carving on the leg and frames consisting of the usual Adelphi detail; strings of a bell-like flower, for example, or plain straight fluted lines; but mahogany chairs are not common and are no more typical of the Adam vogue than painted chairs would be typical of Chippendale. In fact, in the series of books of designs in which the Adelphi published their triumphs mahogany furniture is never mentioned. Accordingly, the collector is faced with the question why so much of the furniture that is commonly regarded as typical 'Adam' is not in the painted and gilded fashion but is furniture of the dining-room type, made in plain mahogany and often not to be described as light.

One answer to this question appears to be simple. When the Adelphi started in business in the 1760's all first-class furniture was made of mahogany. The new taste had to be 'sold' to the public. It is true that already there was a trend towards the lightness which was seen in the late 'French taste' of Chippendale and was the inspiration of the Hepplewhite manner; but painted furniture was a novel departure. The full implication of the Adam theory which might, and did, result in whole rooms showing not one vestige of natural wood, was too great a change to be made all at once; and for furniture intended for the dining-room, where a certain formality and dignity were seemly, mahogany was very suitable. The 'classical' touch could readily be applied to dining-room models in the details of their carved decoration.

The photograph on page 87 shows a very fine marble-topped mahogany side-table which is light not only in its decoration but in its lines. The design of its reeded legs and the Greek honeysuckle decoration which runs along its frieze bring out very clearly the method used by the Adelphi designers in introducing their classical manner.

Incidentally, the Adam side-tables were separate pieces, though flanked sometimes by pedestal cupboards which normally were crowned by 'classical' urns. They were not sideboards in the modern sense. A little later on Hepplewhite, for one, was making sideboards proper in which the wing-cupboards were part of the whole; and the Sheraton sideboard on the same lines is a familiar model.

Summing up, Adam furniture in carved mahogany belongs to the early Adelphi phase, though the usual qualification is needed to a general statement of this kind when dating individual examples. Fine mahogany pieces were made at a later date, no doubt, to carry out some special order, and the fact has always to be borne in mind that the fashionable models of a given era were copied extensively by contemporary makers for some years after they first appeared.

Painted furniture of Adam design is another story; and the subject is reserved for the next chapter together with the work of 'the Hepplewhite School' which flourished after George Hepplewhite's death. This method of obtaining the desired effect was the logical outcome of the Adelphi theory, and the painted, not the mahogany, pieces must be regarded as being representative 'Adam'. The representative Adam style conjures up pictures of tinted ceilings, relief-mouldings in graceful lines, marble mantel-pieces, Flaxman medallions and side-tables painted in white and gold. There was a large element of sham about it. What pretended to be wood was often not wood but a composition of size, resin and whiting. What pretended to be carving was often not carving but a clever mechanically-cast reproduction. The mahogany furniture is entirely different: there is nothing at all of the sham about it. For practical purposes, it must be admitted, the 'dining-room' models need large rooms: they look very impressive in Council chambers or apartments of a similar type where the tone required is a formal dignity. They are fine examples of stately furniture. For the average collector the greater interest in Adam mahogany lies in smaller articles such as dressing-cabinets. In this type of piece Adelphi design is distinguished by the combination of classical details of decoration, such as paterae or bands of fluting, with a slightly stiff architectural feeling discernible in the whole composition. In Hepplewhite pieces of the same general type one would look for graceful curves.

The Adelphi style, like other styles, was not always true to its typical manner. The collection at the Victoria and Albert museum contains an interesting example of the work of Robert Adam in the earlier stages of his career. The piece is a large upholstered sofa designed by Adam in 1765. 'Classical' details in its decoration are combined with extremely clumsy legs which begin in the form of the bodies of cherubs and terminate in animals' paws.

Robert Adam died in 1792, but Adam influence on decoration was still strong at the end of the century.

THE HEPPLEWHITE STYLE

It is not surprising that some confusion exists on the subject of George Hepplewhite and the 'Hepplewhite style'. For one thing, the phrase the 'Hepplewhite style' has been widely used in two different senses. In the second place there are gaps in our knowledge concerning both the man himself and the date of some of the work that is ascribed to him.

The year of George Hepplewhite's birth is not known; nor is the date when he came to London. Even the spelling of his name is uncertain: the form Heppelwhite is often used. It has been stated that he was apprenticed to Gillow, but this again is not established. The known facts are that he was resident in London in 1768 and that he died in 1786. The well-known *Guide* (*The Cabinet-Maker*

TYPICAL HEPPLEWHITE 'SHIELD-BACK' CHAIR

93

and Upholsterer's Guide) was published by his widow, Alice Hepplewhite, in 1788–89. Thereafter the business, a prosperous concern, was carried on by A. Hepplewhite and Co. In point of fact the posthumous *Guide* constitutes the sole existing authority for labelling any piece of furniture 'Hepplewhite'. The style of George Hepplewhite is an inference from the book published two years after his death.

The publication was a commercial success, and the painted furniture of A. Hepplewhite and Co. advertised in the book had a large following. The japanning and painting of chairs was described in the *Guide* as a 'new and very elegant fashion' which had 'arisen within these few years', and this statement was published in 1788 and was probably written a year or two earlier. The designs in the *Guide* possess characteristics that constitute a definite style, and these individual methods and mannerisms are also present in mahogany furniture that certainly belongs to much earlier years and is now generally regarded as 'Hepplewhite'. The disputed point is the earliest date at which this mahogany furniture was designed and made. The balance of evidence, in the opinion of the writer, points to the middle of the 1760's; but the only positive statement which is possible is that this furniture was certainly made between that time and the date, some years before Hepplewhite's death, when the painting and japanning of chairs and settees could be described to the public at large in the *Guide* as a 'new and very elegant fashion'.

Accordingly, the collector has to distinguish between two quite distinct classes of furniture both of which are covered by 'the Hepplewhite style'—the carved mahogany made at the time when Hepplewhite was himself designing, and the painted and decorated type of furniture which was the new vogue at the time of his death and was exploited by A. Hepplewhite and Co. and by the school of makers who followed the *Guide*. The features common to both classes constitute what are commonly accepted as the characteristics of the Hepplewhite manner, and the keynote of this Hepplewhite manner is a combination of daintiness of touch with a great fondness for graceful curves.

The period 1765 to 1800 is a difficult one for the student of furniture. There were three great designers whose work overlaps, Adam, Hepplewhite and Thomas Sheraton, and three fashions which also overlap,—mahogany, satinwood and painted decoration. It helps, however, to clear the picture if two important facts are remembered—that satinwood, introduced about 1760, had become a fashionable wood by, approximately, the year 1770, and that the vogue of painted chairs and sofas (as distinct from the painted work of Adam) started soon after 1780. To avoid confusion this painted furniture is reserved for mention in the next chapter: the present chapter deals only with the mahogany furniture in the style ascribed to Hepplewhite himself many years before painted chairs were announced as a new and elegant fashion. The Hepplewhite mahogany furniture forms a link with the later work of Chippendale and is greatly influenced by Adam teaching in the details of its decoration.

George Hepplewhite was primarily a designer of chairs. Numberless chairs are labelled 'Hepplewhite', and perhaps in this case a special warning is necessary against the old belief that certain items of decoration are a proof that the chair was designed by Hepplewhite and presumably made in Hepplewhite's workshops. The statement used to be made, for example, that a small decoration in the back of a chair consisting of a sheaf of three or more wheat-ears is a certain mark of Hepplewhite's hand; and the same has been said of the shield-shaped back which is illustrated on page 93. Neither of these two statements is sound. The bundle of wheat-ears was used by others, and the shield-shaped back is certainly a design that was favoured also by the Adam brothers. If there is any one hall-mark of Hepplewhite decoration it is the introduction in chair-back design of a plume of Prince of Wales' feathers, for we know that the designer was an ardent Whig and it may well be that this Party badge was an item that he was fond of employing. There may, of course, be certain pieces where the cumulative evidence that Hepplewhite made them is sufficiently strong to satisfy the expert; but in the ordinary case 'a Hepplewhite chair' can only mean a chair in the Hepplewhite style, and that means a chair that is seen to display those characteristics of design and manner of which George Hepplewhite was the leading exponent. The question which the collector must be able to answer is 'How do I recognise the Hepplewhite manner?', and, so far as mahogany furniture is concerned, this question presents no serious difficulty except in some particular cases.

The Hepplewhite style in mahogany chairs has several distinctive characteristics. The first concerns the height of the back which is generally lower, sometimes by inches, than the height that was normal in Chippendale models. This results at times in a stunted appearance; but in any case the height is a certain indication that the chair belongs to the Hepplewhite era if the other characteristics are present. The general design will be slim and graceful, the legs will normally be straight but tapered, and curves will be the feature of the back and arms. The tapering legs may be square or round, and usually carry some carved decoration of an unobtrusive and delicate type. It is typical of the square legs that they are tapered only on the inside edge. (In furniture in the Chippendale style the tapered leg is exceedingly rare.) The best known shapes of the curved backs are the shield-shape, shown on page 93, the oval, the heart, the wheel-back design, and the 'saddle-back'. The wheel-back design is the most admired, and the most familiar, perhaps, is the shield-back. Curves often extend to the seat itself, the level dipping from the sides to the middle; and if the front of the framing is serpentine-shaped, this is a mark of superior work; but in almost all cases graceful curves are a *sine qua non* of Hepplewhite design in chairs and sofas. It is exceptional to find in the *Guide* a chair with a back of rectangular design. Such a chair might resemble a Sheraton chair very closely in the shaping of its back and legs (see page 109); but the distinction between the two would only be difficult if in each case the chair was made of mahogany and did not possess arms.

The shield-back chair shown in the photograph is based on a design in the *Guide* and is both carved and inlaid in satinwood. Indications of its relatively late date (1790) are seen in its reeded legs and 'thimble' toes.

The carved (or inlaid) decoration is always a point to note, whether it be the detail on the slender legs or the design contained in the frame of the back. Hepplewhite, it is quite clear, was greatly influenced by the Adam brothers, and his carving is full of 'classical' touches. The Greek honeysuckle, narrow fluting, little ornaments of pointed leaves, small oval or round paterae and tapering strings of husks or flowers are, one and all, 'Adelphi' details. They would naturally appeal to a dainty taste, and Hepplewhite used them with very great judgment, adding small touches of his own fancy which never lost sight of his main objective —the simple and graceful effect of the whole. A little half-wheel at the base of the back, as seen in the chair on page 93, is one particular Hepplewhite fancy; and the anthemion or Greek honeysuckle was one of his favourite 'classic' items. In some chairs the whole of the back-design is a single theme—an urn or a lyre (both of these typical Adam designs) or his well-known Prince of Wales' feathers. There are also two points of basic design which, taken in conjunction with the other features, stamp chairs and sofas with the Hepplewhite mark. One is the attractive shaping

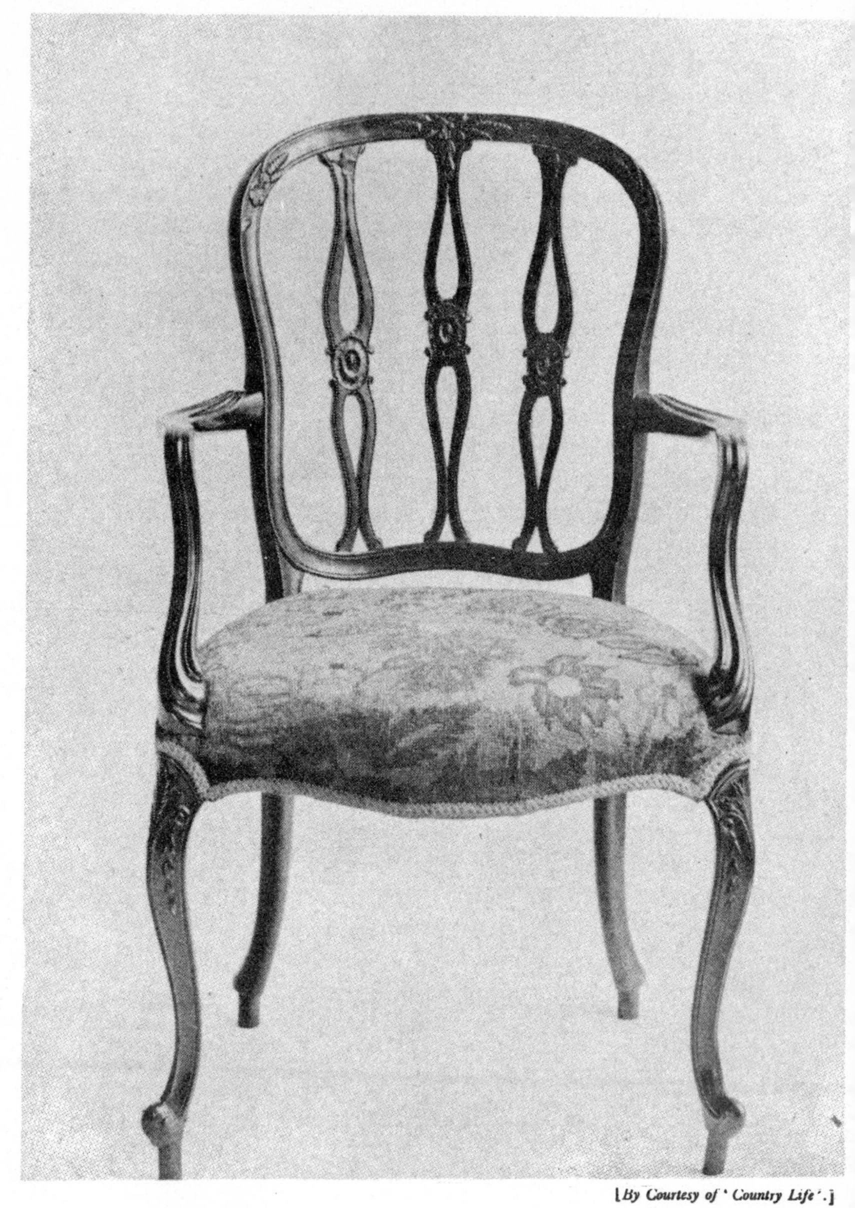

[By Courtesy of 'Country Life'.]

HEPPLEWHITE ARM-CHAIR IN THE 'FRENCH' STYLE (*circa* 1770) 98

of the arms, as seen in the chair illustrated on page 98: they sweep down from the back to the *front* of the seat in a single line and are always treated with special care, expensive of wood but full of grace. The other point concerns the gap that is left between the seat and the base of the shield or oval or other design that is hinged, so to speak, on the back-uprights. It can be taken as almost universally true that in chairs that belong to the Hepplewhite style the lowest part of the back-design is not joined to the seat-frame, as it is in the earlier splat method. The photographs illustrate this point also.

The Hepplewhite leg was not always straight. He also designed in the French taste, using a slender cabriole leg for chairs, sofas and small pieces such as light tables. From about the year 1765 onwards the style in France was becoming lighter: the process of change from the 'Louis Quinze' to the 'Louis Seize' was already resulting in simpler lines which would naturally appeal to Hepplewhite's taste. His French type of chair and settee is usually upholstered: the backs of the chairs are saddle-shaped, and the back of the sofas, which are long and narrow, show flowing curves in unbroken line from end to end of the whole piece. There is only a superficial resemblance to Chippendale's work in the French taste which, apart from other points, is more solid in build and has not the same very simple appearance. The photograph on page 98 shows a Hepplewhite arm-chair in his French style (*circa* 1770).

In furniture other than chairs and sofas Hepplewhite design is similarly marked by a preference for the curved line and a touch of refinement, difficult to describe, in the decoration and the finish. Small tables with long slim cabriole legs (but not claw-and-ball feet) repeat the delicate style of his 'French' chairs. In pieces of the cabinet type the liking for curves is particularly marked by a shape of foot which is characteristic and constitutes a rather special clue in recognising the Hepplewhite manner. This 'French' foot, a sloping bracket, as seen in the photograph on page 101, is usually a fairly safe Hepplewhite 'mark' in mahogany cabinets, book-cases or chests-of-drawers. The unobtrusive use of inlay is also a special point to be noted in distinguishing Hepplewhite from Sheraton design. The dark tones of a mahogany sideboard or similar piece are sometimes relieved by narrow lines of a lighter wood such as satinwood or sycamore, but when Sheraton used the same method the decoration is usually less subdued. This very quiet use of inlay is not, however, confined to Hepplewhite, and the collector who is seeking the Hepplewhite touch has to put more reliance on other features. It is now believed that even Hepplewhite was surpassed in the taste and restraint of his use of inlay by a contemporary designer, Thomas Shearer, whose name has never become so well known as that of his famous friend and rival. Beautiful sideboards in inlaid mahogany were made by both. A note on Shearer is on page 133.

The china-cabinet shown in the photograph is bow-fronted, and illustrates the slender shaping and the sloping 'French' feet that are characteristic of Hepplewhite design. The decoration below the cornice is known as the 'pear-drop' pattern.

As noticed in the case of chairs, Adam details of decoration are again common in Hepplewhite designs for the larger pieces of furniture; but the general lines of his book-cases or cabinets are not marked by the architectural air that characterises Adam productions. In designing his models Hepplewhite aimed at an elegance of effect that is distinguishable from the effect achieved by the more formal Adelphi handling. A Hepplewhite mahogany book-case may have Adam 'marks' in its decoration, but a mahogany book-case designed by the Adelphi will not possess the Hepplewhite touch.

101 CHINA CABINET (*circa* 1785)

Most people, including the average dealer, like to be able to label a piece of furniture of the second half of the 18th century as Chippendale, Adam, Hepplewhite or Sheraton. Museums naturally are more cautious, and in doubtful cases they are content with the label 'mid-18th century' or 'late 18th century'. The difficulty of assigning labels is noted in the following chapter in connection with inlaid mahogany pieces, such as the china-cabinet illustrated on page 101, which combine Hepplewhite and Sheraton features. In dealing with furniture made at a time when the borrowing of designs was common practice it is not easy to draw a fair line between overstatement and understatement of the difficulty of distinguishing styles. In many cases it is quite simple; in others the task of 'placing' a given piece as belonging definitely to a particular style demands a close attention to the special mannerisms which are recognised by expert opinion to be typical of each master. In the case of Hepplewhite the collector must watch for this fine designer's love of curves, the refined and unobtrusive touch which characterises his line and his inlay, and the special marks of his chair designs.

HYBRID DESIGNS

The common use by famous designers of features in the work of other designers which happened to appeal to their own taste is not the same thing as the mixture of styles which results, especially in country-made pieces, in what may be called 'hybrid' designs.

At the time when Chippendale's partnership with Rannie was dissolved (1766) there had come into existence a large number of able craftsmen all over the country who were making furniture in the Chippendale style. In the case of chairs the straight square leg was now the customary pattern in general, but the shaping of the back would be likely to vary, since provincial makers would naturally be inclined

ELM-WOOD COUNTRY-MADE CHAIR OF HYBRID DESIGN

to incorporate details of outline and decoration intended to be in the London fashion, and the 'latest' in London was always changing. The London makers did the same thing, so that furniture of hybrid design was made both in humble and in finer quality. The collector should not be surprised, therefore, when he comes across chairs which cannot be classed as belonging to any single style but combines elements of more than one, and have characteristics of Chippendale design mingled with those of Hepplewhite or Adam.

A country-made chair that is frequently found is illustrated on page 103. The reader will notice that its cresting-rail is of the shape that is known as 'camel back'; that its square legs are very slightly tapered; that the splat in its back reaches down to the seat, and that its general appearance is strong and sturdy. Chairs of this design, varying in the splat, were made in mahogany, chestnut and elm, some of them plain like the one illustrated and others (the finer ones made of mahogany) having carved detail in the back-design.

These chairs are of the standard Chippendale height (though they look lower) and have often been labelled 'Chippendale' chairs. They are also frequently described as 'Hepplewhite' chairs on the strength of the camel-back cresting-rail which was the precursor of the shield-back pattern, and also on account of the slight taper in their legs and the wheat-ear design that appears occasionally in the carved decoration at the top of the back. Again, finely finished mahogany specimens are sometimes labelled 'Adam' chairs, on account, apparently, of the classical detail that is found in some cases in the vase-shaped splat. Experts would quarrel with each of these labels. These chairs are too square and sturdy in build to be in accordance with the dainty manner which we are entitled to associate with the Hepplewhite style, and the incorporation of some Adelphi detail is, alone, no mark of Adam design. On the other hand it is quite natural that chairs of hybrid design should be made. There is nothing strange in country craftsmen incorporating some 'latest' details in sturdy models of their own making; and again, in the case of the finer examples, it would not be unnatural for firms such as Gillow to produce chairs having mixed features. The collector who has studied the styles of the masters can form his own judgment in such a case as to how these pieces should be described.

CHAPTER 9

The Georgian Period. IV

PAINTED FURNITURE AND THOMAS SHERATON

THE vogue of painted furniture was at its height in the twenty years from 1780 to 1800. It was started in the 1760's by the Adam brothers in order to produce light-coloured furniture that accorded with their over-all schemes of interior decoration in the pseudo-classical style. In Adam designs painting was used in two ways. One was to cover the whole surface of the wood, usually a soft-wood such as birch or beech, with a varnish-paint in, say, green or white, and then to pick out this plain background in gold or to paint it in colours with 'classical' decoration. The varnish-paint treatment was known as 'japanning', and it has to be distinguished from the term 'japanning' as used in the early part of the century when it referred to oriental or home-made lacquer, a distinct and far more lasting process. The second method in Adam designs was to paint direct on satinwood, the painting taking the place of inlay. Satinwood from the West Indies became generally available about 1770, and was in great demand from that time onwards.

Both methods of painting were used effectively by the Adam brothers in models such as the side-tables intended to stand under pier-glasses. The underframings of these tables may be gilded all over, or painted in white or some soft colour picked out in gold. The semi-circular top is often of marble, but if the table is of satinwood, it is painted with round or oval medallions framed by the delicate swags and festoons of typical 'Adelphi' drawing.

The next development of the 'painted' vogue was its application to chairs and sofas described as a recent and very elegant fashion in the Hepplewhite *Guide* of 1788, two years after George Hepplewhite's death. This use of painting was exploited successfully by the Hepplewhite school, the mass of craftsmen who followed the *Guide*. The Hepplewhite manner as described in reference to mahogany chairs holds good as regards general design, but the chairs and sofas of the new fashion were made of beechwood 'japanned' and painted. The painted 'bar-backed' sofa mentioned in the *Guide* had a back which, instead of being curved and upholstered, consisted of four or five shield-back designs linked together in a long row. Incidentally the seats were usually caned, the fashion being to use loose cushions of a colour to match the frame-work. In general this painted work was fragile and not of a kind to wear well. Specimens in their present condition have generally lost their original attraction of brightness and colour.

Both methods, painting direct on satinwood (or sometimes on copper let into the panel) and the painting of designs on japanned soft-woods, were also employed by Thomas Sheraton, the last of the famous 'Period' designers.

Whatever else may be said about Sheraton, he was definitely a designer of the front rank, and his character is an important point in as much as it sheds a light on his style. He was born about 1750, and in his youth he was a Baptist preacher and a writer of tracts as well as an ardent student of drawing. Undoubtedly he was a fine draughtsman, and he was ready to lecture the world on perspective. He was also well grounded in cabinet-making, although probably he never had shops of his own. The first edition of his *Drawing Book* (*The Cabinet-Maker and Upholsterer's Drawing-Book*) was published in London in 1791, the second edition in 1793–4, and the third in the year 1802. His friend Adam Black describes him in London as living in an obscure street and looking like 'a worn-out Methodist minister, with thread-bare black coat'. Black also mentions that Sheraton 'had been a cabinet-maker', and he makes it clear that he was very poor in spite of the reception given to his book which apparently went very well with the Trade. He died in 1806.

There has been great argument as to the date at which Thomas Sheraton first came to Town. Did he come to London from Stockton-on-Tees in 1790, the year before his Drawing-Book was published, or did he arrive some ten years earlier? The writer believes in the earlier date. We are given the names of cabinet-makers numbering no fewer than 522 who subscribed in advance to the first edition of his book, and there are various indications in the Drawing-Book itself of an intimate knowledge of the work of the London cabinet-makers. These facts seem hardly consistent with the theory that the book was the work of a draughtsman from the provinces who had only recently arrived in Town.

However that may be, the man was an artist; and there were current modes in the world of furniture that must have appealed to him very strongly. There was Shearer, the apostle of simplicity and restraint in the use of inlay on a mahogany background. There was the Adam fashion in full swing. There was the Louis Seize style of the French Court with its dainty air of refined elegance. It is quite clear that Sheraton borrowed all round; but he does not usually acknowledge his debt. Thomas Sheraton was a narrow man, very ready to quote a religious text, extremely confident of his own ability and less than generous to other designers. He is always teaching with a lofty air. He mingles the advice of an authority on perspective with the exhortations of a Baptist tract. He remarks concerning the Hepplewhite *Guide* that some of the designs are 'not without merit' but unlikely to compete with 'the newest taste' which he, Sheraton, was advertising. To the collector, however, the important point in the character of Sheraton, is his belief in himself as a strict and austere master of drawing; for this had perceptible effects on his line.

The normal conception of the Sheraton style is related entirely to inlaid work. It is probably represented by a mahogany sideboard with slim tapered legs and with lines or fans or ovals of satinwood inlay; or else by a satinwood semi-circular table decorated with inlay in darker woods or with painted designs on its top and its legs. This is a fairly correct impression of the general run of Sheraton designs if his japanned soft-wood work is ignored. Indeed, so many of this designer's models have been reproduced in later days, especially sideboards and smaller pieces such as knife-boxes, tea-caddies and light tables, that most Sheraton types are very familiar. It will be noted, however, that mahogany sideboards of a somewhat similar general appearance were designed and made by Shearer and Hepplewhite. The task of the collector is to be able to recognise, wherever it exists, the distinctive touch of Thomas Sheraton.

Probably the key to the distinctive note in Sheraton outline is the Puritan element in the designer's character. In his line there is always a touch of severity. He liked straight lines, and was critical about the use of curves, and preached in writing against the tendency which he observed in others to mis-apply curves in their designs. This is seen most clearly in Sheraton's chairs. He has been called the pioneer of the straight-back chair in contrast to the prevalent Hepplewhite curves. He would not have approved of the Hepplewhite sofa. When he uses the shield-back shape for a chair, the top of the crest is slightly flattened, and the general shape of his backs is rectangular. Again, in arm-chairs his arms do not curve all the way from the back-uprights to the front of the seat-frame as they do in the

SHERATON ARM-CHAIRS IN PAINTED WOOD (*circa*) 1790

typical Hepplewhite manner: the supports to the arms of the chairs are straight,—they run straight upwards from the seat. Typical Sheraton line is illustrated by the two painted chairs at page 109. Apart from the straight-line form as a whole and particularly the line of the arm-supports, the chief point to note in the chairs illustrated is the rail at the base of the back-design. The rail is clear of the seat of the chair, and this point is an outstanding feature of Sheraton chairs. The photograph on page 116 shows changes that he made at a later date—the second half of the 1790's,—round turned legs in place of square, lattice-splats in the back-design and a cresting-rail that is noticeably broader; but the general rectangular shaping remains.

In his dining-room sideboards of inlaid mahogany and in his larger pieces such as book-cases, which may be either of mahogany or of satinwood veneer, the touch of severity in Sheraton outline is much less obvious than it is in his chairs. It does not imply that he never used curves: he approved greatly of the serpentine swell for the front shaping of sideboards and cabinets. Even so, his objection to the use of curves which were 'unsupported' (his own phrase) can be a useful clue among other factors when Sheraton design is in dispute. The photograph of a sideboard on page 112 pictures a particularly simple model with exceptionally quiet inlay, but the distinctly Sheraton outline is there.

His second general characteristic lies in the style of his decoration. Sheraton decoration is dainty, but not with the daintiness of George Hepplewhite which results in an air of quiet refinement, nor with the daintiness of Adam decoration which conveys an impression of chaste coolness. His touch of severity ends with his outline: Sheraton decoration is pretty. The pretty kind of daintiness is perceptible even in his dining-room models, as witness his mahogany sideboards inlaid with satinwood and the familiar slope-front Sheraton knife-box. In all the rest of his work it is striking.

He excelled at boudoir or drawing-room furniture. Many designs in the *Drawing-Book* have titles such as 'A Lady's Work-Table', 'A Lady's Cabinet', 'A Conversation Chair' or 'A Lady's Cabinet-Writing-Table'. To get his effects he used satinwood freely, which in itself is a dainty wood, and the decoration is either painted or is carried out in coloured inlay, but, whether it is drawn on a satinwood background or is a painted design on japanned beechwood, its pretty manner is a constant feature. A flat tapered leg will have a string of blossom; a round leg will be wreathed in a spiral of flowers; the top of a table or the front of a 'commode' will have a central scheme of coloured medallions, even sometimes a Wedgwood plaque, framed in a setting of ribbons and roses. A pretty taste in swags and knots, festoons and garlands and suchlike detail is a leading feature of Sheraton patterns. He paid great attention to small models. Delicate mirrors for dressing-tables, ladies' work-tables and similar pieces were designed by him in great variety. He also made 'combination' pieces, but these little tables or small cabinets with washstand, mirror and dressing-table fittings were not peculiar to Sheraton, as has sometimes been stated to be the case. Small dressing-room furniture was in great demand and was designed by Hepplewhite, Shearer and others as well as by Sheraton himself.

On the whole it can be said that Sheraton's line and his decorative patterns are distinctive in most cases. The collector should have no particular trouble in distinguishing a Sheraton 'bar-back' sofa from a 'bar-back' sofa in the Hepplewhite manner; nor should he be puzzled by a satin-wood table whether it is decorated with inlay or painting. In the one case the straight-line shaping would be the determining factor; in the other the style of the decoration. A photograph of a Sheraton 'Pembroke' table inlaid with satinwood and other woods is given on page 114. Even in

SHERATON SIDEBOARD

the small bed-room furniture, the Sheraton touch is often clear. This is not to say that there are not models which set very difficult problems indeed if the question at issue goes further than that of their approximate date. A fine and important cabinet-bookcase carried out in veneers of mahogany and satinwood is the sort of piece that might be difficult to 'place' as being definitely in Sheraton's style. It might combine Adam details of decoration with Hepplewhite shaping of the pediment or the feet and a general impression of Sheraton taste. The amateur collector can give it a date—an approximate date within a margin of years, but to go beyond that may demand not only great experience but knowledge of a very detailed kind. As already indicated in previous chapters, it is idle to pretend that every piece of old English furniture can be ascribed definitely to a named style or assigned to a very precise date. In a given case it is quite possible that the greatest expert—and the greater the expert, the less dogmatic—would hesitate either to ascribe it definitely to the Hepplewhite or the Sheraton style or to tie himself within a few years to the date when the cabinet was designed and made. On the other hand there may be points of construction or points concerning the woods used which determine the question at issue for certain. West Indian satinwood, for example, differs from satinwood of the East Indies, and it is known that the latter was not imported before a certain date in the 1790's. For ordinary purposes it is enough to recognise in the problem piece the characteristics of the styles that meet there and to give it a date within a certain margin.

So much importance was attached at this period to the choice of woods for veneers and for inlay that Sheraton practice is worth noting. For veneers, satinwood, sycamore and chestnut were the woods that Sheraton mainly used. In the inlay of his normal sideboard the background of

SHERATON PEMBROKE TABLE (*circa* 1790)

carefully selected mahogany was relieved by lines or bands of holly and fan-shaped angles of satinwood. Other woods used for lines and bands were ebony, kingwood, tulipwood, rosewood, and sycamore stained with oxide of iron which is often referred to as 'harewood' or 'eyrewood'. In Sheraton knife-boxes the circle or star on the inside of the sloping front is inlaid in boxwood and ebony. In designs for the middle of panels or tables the normal woods used are green holly and chestnut.

Originality is the final point on which doubts have been raised about Thomas Sheraton, for critics say, and no one can deny, that there is no element in his designs which he could not have borrowed from existing vogues. It is agreed, however, that his style was distinctive; and in the case of at least two of his models he may have been the originator of the type. One of these is the hanging wardrobe, and the other is the sideboard in the modern sense. The case of the sideboard is open to doubt. It is possible that he was the first designer to combine in a single piece the side table and pedestal-cupboards which were familiar to Adam; but the Adams themselves or Hepplewhite or Shearer may actually have been the first to do this. He has also been credited with the 'Pembroke' table, a small table with flaps supported by brackets, as shown in the photograph; but this design appears also in the Hepplewhite *Guide*.

The change in the shaping of the Sheraton chair towards the end of the century has already been mentioned and is illustrated by the mahogany and satinwood arm-chair shown in the photograph on page 116. In the late 1790's the square tapered leg was superseded generally by the round turned leg, and the 'thimble-toe', seen in the photograph on page 109, was ousted from favour by the 'peg-top' foot (shown in the picture of the later chair) which became so popular in Victorian days. Other features of the change were a decrease in height, the broadening of the top-rail of

[*By courtesy of "Country Life."*]

SHERATON CHAIR: LATER STYLE (*circa* 1795)

the back and the placing of the splats in the back-design. In the later fashion the splats ran sideways from upright to upright. The changes which affected other models as well as chairs were the use of rosewood in place of mahogany (though mahogany never went out of fashion) and the free employment of brass ornament. Brass trellis for bookcase-fronts and brass rails at the back of sideboards had been in favour for a number of years, but in the late 1790's inlay as well began to be carried out in brass, usually in the form of thin lines. The lion's-head handle also appeared in these last years of the 18th century. The handles of the Sheraton wine-cooler shown on page 118 are of this type. The top of the wine-cooler is inlaid with thin lines of satinwood which run diagonally from the eight corners to an oval in the middle containing the usual shell design.

The third edition of the *Drawing-Book*, published in 1802, contains many designs which are strongly influenced by the French features of the 'Empire' furniture which is the subject of the following chapter.

. . . . . .

In the opening years of the 19th century there was a reversion to furniture of heavy build. The furniture of the Hepplewhite-Sheraton epoch is noticeable for its light weight as compared both with that of the Regency style which followed it and with that of the Chippendale era which preceded it. This point is well illustrated by the particular case of dining tables. The Chippendale table, as generally pictured, is a heavy table with cabriole legs. Chippendale, of course, made dining tables with straight legs also, but even these, with their square legs, present a relatively weighty appearance. At the other end of the epoch the Regency style, as noted in the following chapter, produced solid tables with massive central supports, and

SHERATON WINE-COOLER (*circa* 1790)

this markedly heavy type of design persisted in the Victorian era. In contrast with these the typical table of the interim period was a light table in four parts: two middle sections of oblong shape and two semi-circular end-pieces. The parts could be joined by small brass fittings, or the ends, detached, would be used as side-tables. Invariably the legs were tapered and the general appearance was one of lightness. From the point of view of the modern collector who is seeking a mahogany dining-room table, the table of the Hepplewhite-Sheraton epoch is the best model for which to look.

CHAPTER 10

The Georgian Period. V

'REGENCY'

'English Empire' is a term so often used with reference to a phase of Regency furniture that it may be as well to mention it. Actually neither 'Regency' nor 'English Empire' is a very accurate name. The future King George the Fourth did not become Prince Regent until February, 1811, but 'Regency' embraces the furniture made from about 1800 to 1820. Similarly, Napoleon did not declare himself Emperor of the French until 1804, but the French 'Empire' style was in process of development from the days of the Revolution onwards and had assumed its definite characteristics by the year 1800. 'English Empire' is a name sometimes used for the furniture of the so-called Regency period which was inspired by the new French fashion.

During the years of the Directoire which followed immediately on the French revolution Paris 'went classical'. The movement was inspired by the idea that the new Republic would emulate the glories of ancient Athens, Sparta and Rome. Children were given classical names. Ladies in artistic circles gave Roman dinner-parties at which gentlemen recited Greek poems. Furniture assumed ancient Greco-Roman lines. Tables were supported by columns surmounted by human half-figures (caryatides), and all the familiar details of 'classical' decoration were brought once more into use. The wars of Bonaparte added their quota. Wreaths of bay-leaf, significant of victory, took their place besides Roman *fasces*, and the Egyptian campaign of 1798 added sphinxes, animals and figures of Isis to the list of items in the decorative schemes. Bonaparte, as Consul, encouraged the fashion and the 'Empire' style was firmly established. English designers, not omitting Sheraton in his final phase, borrowed those features of 'French Empire' which suited the trend of Regency taste.

Books dealing with Old English Furniture used to cease abruptly at the year 1800 on the ground that no furniture after that date was worthy to be classed with the 'Period' styles. The Regency taste, taken as a whole, was very extravagant in outline and colour. Others would prefer to say 'rich' and 'romantic'. The following are short descriptions of some of the samples included in the collection of Regency furniture exhibited in the Royal Pavilion at Brighton in August, 1946:—

Side-table of rosewood mounted with satinwood and supported by carved Chinese dragons. (1817).

Cabinet of imitation bamboo, with yellow marble top and ormolu gallery. (About 1802).

A kingwood writing-table, on standards, decorated with ormolu ornaments, and lions' heads on the gilt fluted frame, and decorated with trusses richly carved and gilt; the stretchers covered with velvet.

Rosewood Pier Tables with shelves on the top, decorated with brass mouldings, the frieze and column richly carved and gilt, red silk backs, and on plinths of imitation porphery.

Shell-shaped silver lacquer chairs.

Pier Tables of ebony with richly chased ormolu mounts and red marble tops.

Among the exhibits were also the following:—

Pair of Louis XVI cabinets purchased by King George IV in 1820.

Pair of arm chairs in white and gold, with open honey-suckle backs and goat's-hoof feet. (About 1810).

Sofa-table of Amboyna wood inlaid with brass. (Made in 1816 for the Princess Charlotte).

Rosewood cabinet with wire trellis work. (About 1815).

Thus the Regency period presents a curious mixture. Of the four last-named items there is nothing extravagant about the rosewood cabinet or about the sofa-table of amboyna, which relies entirely on the beauty of its wood. Again, the Louis Seize style of the cabinets was simple in outline, and the French Empire style represented by the pair of white and gold chairs was intended to be severe. There were elements, in fact, in the Regency taste which cannot be 'written off' as inartistic barbarities, and such merits as there are in 'English Empire' should be recognised by the collector.

The new French fashion had considerable effect on Regency designers. The main characteristics of the French style were three—the mixture, already noted, of Greco-Roman and Egyptian decorative forms, the lavish use of gilt-bronze mounts, and its strength. French artists had been in a difficult position. It was not particularly safe to employ in their designs either the soft colours or the delicate lines that savoured of the *ancien régime.* The order of the day was for a style that was harsh, stern and formal. Beauty was not the first consideration: the primary motive was to symbolise in design and decoration the strength of a newly-inspired and victorious nation which would recall the triumphs of ancient Rome. The chairs were based directly on the models of the ancient world. The couches were intended to be severely classical in their simple lines. The legs and feet of animals which supported the tables were derived from patterns unearthed at Pompeii or discovered in Egypt. The griffins with stiffly outstretched wings, the sphinxes and the figures of Isis were all regarded as suitable symbols for the new Republic or, later, Empire. It was all very stilted, massive and pompous, and the metal mountings assisted to achieve a total effect of virility and weight.

Why English designers favoured these patterns at a time when their country was at war with France and the 'Corsican Ogre' was a hated bogey, is a matter that is better left to the historian. The fact remains that this was the case. The strong influence which the Louis Seize style had exercised over Sheraton and his contemporary designers in the early part of the 1790's was entirely submerged by the new ideas that were now borrowed from across the Channel. It was all in accord with the reigning taste for colour, strength and extravagant shapes. Sheraton himself in his last years, with a change of taste which is hard to understand, adopted grotesque forms in designs. We read of 'chairs composed of a griffin's head, neck and wings, united by a transverse tie of wood over which is laid a drapery; another whose front is composed of a dog's head and leg, with shaggy mane, joined by a reeded rail'. Thomas Hope, on the other hand, who in 1807 published a book on Household Furniture and Decoration, took a much more strictly classical line in the designs which he founded on the Empire manner. 'English Empire' is something of a mixed dish.

There emerged, however, some chairs and sofas, sofa-tables and dining-room tables which found great favour in American eyes and are not unhonoured in their own country. There are, for example, 'English Empire' chairs in mahogany or rosewood which follow the simple lines of Sheraton models of the late 1790's. Any decoration which they possess is carried out in brass inlay; but the outstanding characteristic which marks the Empire chair is the outward splay of its front legs, as shown in the photograph on page

ARM-CHAIR IN STAINED BEECH-WOOD WITH BRASS MOUNTS (*circa* 1810)

123. A similar curve is seen in the legs of tripod tables of this era, and in the supports of sofa-tables. The most useful arm-chair of the early 19th century is a *bergère* chair with a mahogany or rosewood frame and caning in its back, seat and arms. It is fitted with thick loose cushions and is both comfortable and of pleasing shape. (The Chippendale 'burjar' is an upholstered arm-chair).

The typical table is a weighty piece with a large oval or round top supported by a massive central pillar, the base resting upon four feet mounted in brass in the shape of claws. It is well constructed, and the wood is often fine and beautiful. The sofas, which seem to have been particularly popular with American collectors of 'Old Colonial'*, are sober-looking models, long and large, with their ends shaped in a swan-neck curve, and the usual 'Empire' brass claw-feet. In general construction was first-class, the furniture gives an impression of strength, and the beauty of the wood is sometimes striking. The sofa-table mentioned above, which was made in the year 1816, has a top of golden amboyna-wood not to be surpassed in figure and colour.

* See note on 'Old Colonial Furniture', page 135.

CHAPTER II

Note on the French Epochs

AT various points in its history the style of English furniture was directly affected by French influences. On two occasions this was due to the influx of artisans and skilled craftsmen who had fled from across the Channel to escape from religious persecution. In the other cases it was the result of contact with the fashions of the powerful Courts which ruled France. The Louis Quatorze, Louis Quinze, Louis Seize and the First Empire styles all had effects in various degrees on the Period styles in this country. The collector who knows the characteristics of the French epochs can follow the points at which the influence is seen in the changing vogues of English design.

LOUIS QUATORZE

The long reign of Louis XIV (1643–1715) covered the last years of Charles I, the Commonwealth, the Restoration period and the reigns of William and Mary and Queen Anne.

This is the epoch of the *Grande Monarque*, when for fifty years a despotic king created a court of great magnificence centred round the palace at Versailles. The crown took a hand in developing the arts and crafts. The famous Gobelins factory was by no means confined to tapestry-making. In 1663 it was given the title of 'The Royal Manufactory of Furniture of the Crown', and furniture-designers were treated as artists.

The 'Louis Quatorze' was a solemn and pompous style.

Its features were massive grandeur and sumptuous decoration, in which gilded carving, ormolu (gilded brass) mountings and intricate marquetry played the chief parts. Typical specimens of this palace furniture were large armoires of ebony, console tables with marble tops and under-framings of gilded scroll-work, or 'commodes' enriched by ormolu mounts designed and chased by selected artists. Immense sums of money were spent on these 'meubles de luxe'. The most famous *ébéniste* was André Charles Boulle who specialised in the type of marquetry, known ever since by the name 'Buhl', in which intricate patterns of flowing arabesques are outlined in brass on a background of tortoiseshell (or vice versa) veneered on ebony.

The influence of this style on English work is seen chiefly in two directions—the scrolled leg-work of chairs and of the stands of cabinets in the later years of the Restoration period; and the delicate 'over-all' marquetry in woods which became the fashion for the decoration of walnut furniture in William and Mary and Queen Anne days.

LOUIS QUINZE

The reign of Louis XV (1715–1774) covered the Early Georgian period, the era of Chippendale and the earlier years of the Adam style and the Hepplewhite manner.

The young king was a minor until 1723, and this transitional period, known as the 'Régence', saw a change in the customs of the French aristocracy which immediately affected the style of decoration. The vast galleries of old Versailles were transformed into more intimate salons. The age of *petits appartements* had arrived, and furniture moved from the stately and dignified to a more free and less massive mode. The somewhat gloomy formality of the 'Louis Quatorze' gave way to a vogue of dazzling extravagance. The pursuit of decorative elegance resulted in the 'rococo' style in which the straight line became a thing of the past, and outline and decoration alike ran riot in a profusion of curves. The derivation itself of the term 'rococo' from *rocaille* and *coquaille*, rock-work and shell-work, indicates the kind of elaborate detail that characterised the artistic licence. The carved detail was overloaded and the chased ormolu mountings were overdone. The marquetry was exceedingly complex. Rosewood, king-wood, tulip-wood, and sycamore are the most noticeable of the woods employed, but every type was pressed into service, in its natural state or stained or engraved, which contributed contrasting colours. A typical piece would be a writing-bureau with body and legs shaped in swelling curves, inlaid with a pattern of glowing woods and almost encrusted with glittering mounts.

Both the cabinet work and the metal work were, in themselves, extremely fine, and the names of Jean Francois Oeben, Charles Cressent, Riesener and Caffieri will remain famous for all time. The marquetry work and the chased mountings by these artists have probably never been equalled since in point of marvellous technical skill. Some of the earlier work was more restrained, but in the typical Louis Quinze model the adornment with mountings is over-elaborate and the marquetry work is over-ambitious in an attempt to render pictures in wood. Lacquer panels were also used, and the lacquer process called Vernis-Martin was the great invention of the Louis Quinze period, just as 'Buhl' was that of the Louis Quatorze. It is a point of interest that the famous French *ébénistes* often stamped their signatures on their work; so that identification of the actual maker is possible in the case of fine French furniture far more frequently than in the case of English.

Towards the end of the reign a more simple style which is called 'à la reine', paved the way for the change to 'Louis Seize'.

'Louis Quinze' influence on English furniture is chiefly

to be noted in Chippendale's work. It shows itself in the shaping and detailed carving of his more florid chairs, and sometimes in the outline of his cabinet pieces, and clearly in the case of his rare 'commodes' built entirely in the French taste. It is also noticeable in the carved decoration of the columns and feet of his tripod tables, and in the shape and the chasing of his brass handles.

It was only the later phase of the style, when the curved leg was becoming much lighter, that appealed to, and influenced, George Hepplewhite.

LOUIS SEIZE

The tragic reign of Louis XVI and his Queen, Marie Antoinette, lasted from 1774 to 1793, and the trend towards a lighter form of elegance in decoration and furniture which had been developing for some years before 1774, culminated in a very definite change of style.

The 'Louis Seize' style has been described as simple, but it is only simple by contrast with the 'rococo' style of typical 'Louis Quinze'. In structural form it was certainly more simple, for the extravagant use of curves was abandoned in favour of the straight line. The cabriole leg, when it was retained, became far lighter, and the straight tapered leg was a notable feature of the new fashion. The gilt-bronze mountings, too, were lighter, and, side by side with the marquetry work, small cabinets and other boudoir furniture were now built in plain wood and only adorned by the ormolu mounts. The simplicity of the 'Louis Seize' was the costly and exquisite pseudo-simplicity of an artificial Arcadian setting. Rooms were panelled in soft colours, and slender ovals were much in favour. Plaques of Sèvres porcelain enriched the cabinets; little writing-tables and work-tables exemplified the taste for dainty models, and furniture was often painted white or in delicate blues, or greens or greys. The decoration was pastoral in theme.

Roses were entwined with ribbons and knots, slender and flowery stripes abounded, and shepherd's crooks and rustic scythes were interwoven with lyres and flutes. A delicate type of elegance reigned, and furniture conformed to the general *ensemble*. The style achieved a consummate grace.

The most famous craftsmen were Riesener, *ébéniste* to Marie Antoinette, David Röntgen, and, for ormolu mountings, Pierre Gouthière, whose work has always fetched fabulous prices.

The influence of the 'Louis Seize' on English styles was considerable. How far it affected Adam design is not an easy question to answer, but the trend of French fashion towards greater lightness was certainly an influence with the wealthy patrons for whom the Adelphi designed their houses. In the case of George Hepplewhite's gentle curves the French influence is plain to see. In the case of Sheraton's line it is marked, and the whole style of his painted work was probably inspired by the Louis Seize fashion when he was not drawing on Adam detail.

EMPIRE

The style which followed the French Revolution and is known generally as 'French Empire', is described in Chapter 10.

. . . . . .

The English student of furniture is fortunate in the possession, in London, of two very fine collections of the work of the masters of the French epochs—the Wallace Collection at Hertford House and the Jones Bequest at the Victoria and Albert Museum*. Here can be seen representative pieces by Boulle, Caffieri, Cressent, Riesener, Pierre Gouthière and many others.

* Note. At the time of writing the full collections of old furniture at the Victoria and Albert Museum, South Kensington, are not yet on view again; but the Art Library with its collection of photographs is open to the public.

CHAPTER 12

The Less-known English Makers and Designers

FORTY years ago the average collector had never heard of Edwards and Darly, Ince and Mayhew, William Vile, Robert Manwaring and the rest of the less-known names of 18th century designers and makers. Since then the truth has been widely accepted that Chippendale, Hepplewhite and Sheraton were not responsible for one-tenth of the designs which have been attributed to them, and still more so that makers like Chippendale and Hepplewhite could not have produced more than a small fraction of the total of tables, chairs, cabinets and chests which have been labelled and sold as the work of their shops. The majority of the minor names are only known by reason of the fact that these gentlemen published books of designs, and the tendency of modern research has been to examine these books and other data in order to determine the degree of contribution that was made by their writers to the famous cabinet-work of the time.

This study does not throw any doubt on the point that the few who achieved a lasting fame were truly men of outstanding ability. It does not invalidate the proposition that Chippendale, Hepplewhite, Adam and Sheraton had distinctive styles which are recognisable. It is merely an effort to get at the truth in the light of the knowledge that in the 18th century there was no copyright, that designers borrowed each other's ideas, and that craftsmen copied them freely and widely. It is probable that many a fine piece of furniture for which credit has been given to one of the masters was really the work of a designer or maker, such as William Vile, whose name has remained relatively obscure. The modern collector should know the names of these men, and the influence on design with which each has been credited. The following particulars of the better known of these 'lesser lights' are given in the order of the date of their books.

BATTY LANGLEY

It is probable that the influence of this architect on the furniture of 1740 to 1760 was considerable. Langley started as a landscape gardener. In 1740 he published *The City and Country Builder's and Workman's Treasury of Designs*, which contained some Chinese frets many years before Chippendale, Edwards and Darly and Sir William Chambers entered this field of design. In 1747 he published *Gothick Architecture Improved by Rules and Proportions* which is said to have originated the 'Gothic taste', and he received commissions from Horace Walpole. The shaped oblong panels with rounded corners which characterise his designs for the doors of cabinet-bureaux are a special feature of the furniture of the period 1740–1750.

EDWARDS AND DARLY

Matthias Darly was successful as an engraver, an architect and a caricaturist as well as a designer, and was the engraver of the majority of the plates in the first edition of Chippendale's *Director* of 1754. In the same year Edwards and Darly published their own book entitled *A New Book of Chinese Designs*, which was 'calculated to improve the public taste', and it is probable that it was from Darly that Chippendale derived his knowledge of Chinese ornament.

THOMAS JOHNSON

Johnson, a carver with a business in Holborn, is known

for the books of designs which he published between 1755 and 1761. His drawings for chairs, mirrors, candle-stands, etc. exaggerated the rococo style associated with some of Chippendale's work (notably his mirrors) in mixed Louis Quinze and Chinese shaping.

INCE AND MAYHEW

William Ince was a subscriber to the second edition of Chippendale's *Director*, and in 1762 the partners, who owned a considerable business in Golden Square, published their own book, *The Universal System of Household Furniture*, which consisted of 'above 300 Designs in the most elegant Taste'.

The firm has been described as Chippendale's most faithful imitators. The designs in their book include models in the Louis Quinze, the Gothic and the Chinese tastes, and show a strong leaning towards fret-cut work. They are so closely akin to Chippendale's style that in the case of many models showing fret-cut decoration it is not possible to say that they should be credited to Chippendale rather than to Ince and Mayhew. The firm is mentioned in 1803 (as 'Mayhew and Ince') in Sheraton's list of cabinet-makers.

ROBERT MANWARING

Manwaring was primarily a designer of chairs who in 1765 published a book called *The Cabinet and Chair-Maker's Real Friend and Companion*, or 'The Whole System of Chair making made plain and easy, containing upwards of 100 new and useful designs for all sorts of chairs in the Chinese and Gothic taste'. The drawings were extremely badly executed. Manwaring has been described as Chippendale's principal rival after Ince and Mayhew.

MATTHIAS LOCK

Alone, or together with H. Copeland, this designer published three books of 'Ornaments' in 1768 and 1769, specialising in the frames for pier-mirrors and girandoles.

THOMAS SHEARER

It is very probable that Shearer had a considerable influence on both Hepplewhite and Sheraton design. The slender information which is available concerning him is derived from his nineteen plates of *Designs of Household Furniture* published in 1788, and from the fact that he was commissioned to provide a number of plates for the *Cabinet-maker's London Book of Prices* of which the first edition appeared in 1788 and further editions in 1793 and 1803. This latter fact proves that Shearer was widely recognised as a sound practical craftsman. On the strength of his published drawings he has been described as 'the apostle of simplicity' in the design of mahogany furniture carrying a modicum of satinwood inlay. He was the first man to publish the design of a self-contained sideboard incorporating the wing-cupboards of the earlier pattern of side-table *cum* pedestals. It would be difficult to distinguish his small dressing-table mirrors from those of Sheraton.

THOMAS HOPE

The name of Thomas Hope, architect and author, is particularly associated with the 'English Empire' style. His Book *Household Furniture and Interior Decoration* was published in 1807. The designs are based on the conception of Greco-Roman decoration which was the main element in the French 'Empire' style.

. . . . . .

The following firms published no books.

GILLOW AND CO.

This old Lancaster firm was established by Robert Gillow at the end of the 17th century. The Gillows opened a London office in 1765, an enterprise which they called

'The Adventure to London'. Great interest attaches to their cost-books for the year 1784 and onwards, which exist and contain rough illustrations of their work. These cost-books show that towards the end of the 18th century they were making furniture in the Chippendale and Hepplewhite styles many years after these models were out of date in London fashion. The designs also show that they were much influenced by Adam. They published no book and founded no distinctive style of their own, but established a great reputation as fine craftsmen. The firm came to be better known for its work in the 19th century style.

THE SEDDONS

So far as can be traced, this important firm was founded by George Seddon who in 1754 was one of the subscribers to the first edition of Chippendale's *Director*. Records show that the firm was in a large way of business in Aldersgate Street, London, in 1768, and still more so in 1791, from which date until 1802 the title was changed to Seddon, Sons, and Shakleton. The Seddons are mentioned in Sheraton's list of cabinet-makers in 1803, and were entrusted by King George IV with the re-furnishing of Windsor Castle. It is clear that from the middle of the 18th century onwards they were regarded as most eminent cabinet-makers, and they were doubtless responsible for much of the fine furniture of the period.

WILLIAM VILE AND JOHN COBB

Modern research has drawn attention to the important place occupied by William Vile as a craftsman and designer at the time when Chippendale published the first edition of his *Director* in 1754. He was in partnership with John Cobb and may have been responsible for some of the designs in Chippendale's book. Examples of his work are included in the Royal collections.

CHAPTER 13

Short Notes on Special Subjects

'OLD COLONIAL' FURNITURE

IN the United States of America 'Old Colonial' furniture has always possessed a sentimental attraction, and there are many books that record the adventures of American collectors who have toured their country in search of 'finds'. The term 'Old Colonial' means, or ought to mean, the furniture taken or imported to America by the English and Dutch settlers between the early part of the 17th century and the Declaration of Independence of 1776 which ended the Colonial status of the settlements. It includes the furniture that was made locally from the original models.

The first settlement in Virginia was in 1607; the voyage of the *Mayflower* took place in 1620; Maryland was colonised in 1634; the Dutch settlement of New Amsterdam (later New York) was taken by the English in 1664; and Pennsylvania was 'settled' in 1681. Throughout that century the more well-to-do settlers took some furniture with them and imported more as time went on. The 17th century furniture was of the simplest kind: chests, plain turned chairs with rush seats, stools, tables, settles, an occasional Jacobean court-cupboard and the large Dutch cupboard known as a 'kas'. From the beginning of the 18th century onwards the importation of furniture was continuous. At first in New England the majority of the pieces were of Dutch origin, and the 'high-boy' (our tall-boy) on cabriole legs was highly regarded as a family treasure, but as the century progressed the main flow consisted of mahogany furniture in the prevailing English styles. The Colonial buildings of the time were based on Queen Anne and Georgian architecture, and the 18th century models in furniture followed one another to America in succession. Naturally the colonial craftsmen who copied them very often used native woods, and the advertisements of the local salesmen advertised almost every variety. Windsor chairs were extremely popular.

With American writers the term 'Old Colonial' is apt to be used in a wider sense to include furniture that was made or imported after the date 1776 when the word 'colonial' becomes a misnomer. This is noticeably the case with rocking-chairs which were not made before that date (though rocker-cradles are very much earlier), and with English Empire of the 19th century which seems to have been particularly favoured. The long sofa with brass claw-feet is one example of a favourite piece. It is a commonplace that American culture has always evinced a very special interest in Period furniture of all types whether 'Old Colonial' in the strict sense or imported at a later date.

Among the famous pieces of real 'Old Colonial' which are carefully preserved are Elder Brewster's chair in Pilgrim's Hall, Plymouth; a turned chair of the time of the Mayflower which originally had a rush seat; William Penn's chair in Independence Hall, Pennsylvania—a late Charles II caned model; and the library chair of Benjamin Franklin, a mid-18th century padded-back chair.

'IRISH CHIPPENDALE'

There is a mystery about this title. It refers to a quantity of mahogany furniture made in the reign of George II which has been found in most parts of Ireland.

This furniture is solidly built and extravagant in its use of wood, and seems to consist most largely of side-tables. It has certain characteristics in common. The side-tables often have marble tops and are normally distinguished by 'aprons' of carving on their underframings below the top. They have highly decorated cabriole legs. Favourite central features in the carved 'aprons' are scallop-shells of the Queen Anne tradition or grotesque masks. The carving usually has an effect of flatness, or at any rate it is in great contrast to the sharp carving associated with the Chippendale school. It would be fair to say of the usual example that the line and the general design are ungainly.

It is a nice point which is open to argument whether this furniture was made in Ireland or imported from England. In the latter case it is clearly provincial. The point which seems to be quite evident is that there is no justification whatever for the name 'Chippendale' to appear in its title.

'SPINDLE' FURNITURE

Nests of coffee-tables are the form in which the collector is most likely to come across examples of the spindle-leg furniture that was made in mahogany in the second half of the 18th century. Other models are the tripod wig-stands of the kind which were designed by Chippendale, basin-stands, towel-rails, fire-screens and small occasional tables. They are, of course, examples in a simple and fragile form of the turned-work that was common in the 17th century for the legs of gate-leg tables or the balusters in certain types of chairs (see photograph on page 38). It is not often that these little mahogany pieces can be associated with a particular style, though a small table sometimes suggests the Hepplewhite manner in the curves of its top or of the stretcher that joins its four slim legs. This work is very easy to imitate, and particular attention should be paid to the wood in the matter of its colour and surface-condition.

After about the year 1800 rosewood was used for the coffee-tables as well as mahogany, and the small platforms on which the legs stand began to be of a less simple shape and

CHILD'S ROCKING-CHAIR IN ELM-WOOD (1780-1800)

somewhat ungainly in proportion to the legs. Specimens that are made of mahogany and have plain-shaped feet are to be preferred.

The photograph on this page shows a child's rocking-chair of the late 18th century, made of elm-wood, with spindle balusters in the back.

TYPES OF CLOCKS

There are three classes of clock, or rather of clock-cases, that come within the definition of old furniture—the brass 'bird-cage' or lantern clock, the long-case or 'Grandfather' clock, and the bracket-clock proper intended to stand on a bracket, a table or a mantel. The works or 'movements' of clocks are a separate study; and it is a sound general rule that the date of the movement (which is usually known) is not a safe guide to the date of the case. Clock-makers commissioned their own cases and were slow to accept new-fashioned shapes.

The bird-cage or lantern clock made its first appearance about the year 1620. Its form is familiar—a square brass dial attached to the works which are left uncovered except at the top where they are crowned with a circular brass dome. In a sense this was a bracket clock since, unless it was fastened to the wall at the back, it was made to stand on a wooden bracket and the weights which drove the clock hung down on cords which passed through holes in the wooden platform. The earliest clocks had no pendulum: the pendulum was not introduced until about the year 1660. The dials usually had only one hand until the last years of the reign of Charles II. It was not superseded by the grandfather clock but continued to be made throughout the 18th century, more especially in country districts.

The Grandfather clock first appeared in this country during the reign of Charles II, when the works of the old lantern clock were protected from dust by a square-shaped hood, and the pendulum and cords by a long case. The size of the dial was about 10 inches across, and the shape of the hood was a plain square with a straight-line cornice in the classical style. The corners of the dial outside the circle are filled by ornaments in pierced brass, usually a cherub's head and wings. The first cases were made in oak

LONG-CASE CLOCK IN WALNUT AND MARQUETRY
(*circa* 1720)

140

or chestnut and the finer ones were veneered in walnut. English marquetry-work on the hood and long cases was of a simple type at this stage, and clock-cases of the Restoration period which carry elaborate marquetry-work were probably made by Dutch craftsmen. In the William and Mary and Queen Anne period the long case of the Grandfather clock was a favourite subject for decoration in the intricate marquetry than in fashion; and flower designs and, later, arabesques carried out in contrasted yellows and browns, often cover the whole case. Fine clocks of this type are exquisite examples of English marquetry of the best period and have a high value.

Two changes were made in the reign of Queen Anne. After about the year 1700 the size of the dial was increased from about 10 to about 12 inches across, and the straight-line cornice went out of fashion, the top of the hood being usually surmounted by a long-shaped dome. These domed tops often have three brass spires, of which the commonest form has a ball ornament. Up to this time the dial was a plain square, but a change was made after Queen Anne's reign and a dial with an arch in its top line was the usual shape for the rest of the century. The photograph on page 140 shows this shape of dial, and also illustrates the domed form of the top and the style of Queen Anne marquetry work. Clock-cases faced with English lacquer mostly belong to this post-Anne period.

The next stage was the mahogany case, which does not appear to have come into fashion until the second half of the 18th century. All clocks after 1750 or so have arched tops of some form or other, often of the 'broken pediment' shape, each side of the break being a curved scroll. Fret decoration in the Chippendale style on the frieze or the chamfered edges of the case does not indicate any particular date in the last fifty years of the 18th century, but inlay in the typical Sheraton style is probably later than 1780. In the last quarter of the 18th century the dial was no longer always of brass, but is sometimes enamelled and sometimes painted.

The third type of clock, the bracket-clock proper, is very rare before William and Mary. Examples made in the Dutch Period in marquetry-work are also rare: plain walnut or ebonised wood are more common. Its general outline remained constant during the whole course of the Georgian era, though additional shapes made their appearance in the last phase of the century. It was better suited than the Grandfather clock to the fashionable style of Georgian room. The typical top in the early stages is a flat-topped dome of the type shown in the photograph of the long-case clock, which was sometimes made of pierced brass-work suggesting the title 'basket-top'. It is surmounted by a brass handle. The dial changed to the arched form at the same time as that of the Grandfather clock. The dome-shape top never went out of fashion, but other shapes became popular as well in the last thirty years of the century, and in many mahogany clocks of this period the top of the case is a simple arch that more or less follows the arch of the dial. Fretted designs in the sides are a feature. The feet are either small brackets or balls. In Sheraton's time, when inlay was the fashion, three other shapes were also in use, and the dial is often a plain circle. These three forms are the plain round top, the pointed arch, and the so-called 'balloon' which recalls the shape of an inverted pear.

TYPES OF HANDLES AND LOCK-PLATES

The value of a piece of furniture is increased if it possesses its original handles and lock-plates; but it is frequently the case that the original fittings have been replaced by others which are either old fittings of a later date or modern reproductions. The appearance of old brass can be imitated very successfully by chemical treatment; but when the fittings are of the pierced or chased type, the reproductions are not difficult to distinguish if they have been made by the modern cheap method, for the absence of tool-work is easily discernible. It is useful to know the main types that were in current use in the various periods. Each type was, of course, made in great variety as regards detailed design, but the general lines of the shapes that were in common use at various stages can be distinguished.

Before the time of William and Mary any handles on the doors of cupboards or the fronts of drawers were usually small wooden knobs such as are shown in the photograph of a Jacobean chest on page 28, and any metal fittings such as lock-plates were normally made of hammered iron. The brass handles used for drawers in William and Mary days hung from solid (i.e. not pierced) plates which were often engraved. There were two main shapes: the 'drop' handle such as those shown in the photograph of a Secretaire on page 46, and the handle which consisted of a rather slender brass loop and on a solid shaped plate. These handles were fastened by two flat wires which pierced the front and were bent back flush with the back of the drawer. The drop-handles seen on the Secretaire are the most ornamental handles of that type: in their commonest form the 'drop' was plainly shaped like a pear. The photograph also shows the style of the lock-plates, which were fastened with small brass pins.

Pierced, instead of solid, plates both for handles and locks were introduced towards the end of the reign and were usual in the reign of Queen Anne. The pierced plates were cut in a great variety of designs.

In the middle part of the 18th century the handle was no longer fixed to a back-plate but hung between two 'roses' as shown in the photograph of a Chippendale chest-of-drawers which forms the Frontispiece or the tall-boy on page 82. These 'roses' were bolted through the front of the drawer and secured by nuts screwed on from behind. In furniture of ordinary quality the 'roses' were plain circles and the handles themselves were plain brass loops of the shape seen in these two photographs. In elaborate furniture in the Chippendale style both 'roses' and handles were often shaped on the so-called 'flamboyant' style associated with 18th century French furniture. These latter examples were finished with great care and frequently display exquisite chasing. Imitations that are merely cast from a mould have a non-smooth look that is not easily mistaken for the fine finish achieved by tooling.

In the second half of the 18th century the lock-plate gave way, as a general rule, to a simple brass rim key-hole. Little ivory plates are sometimes used where a dainty effect is specially sought. The drawer-handle of the simple mid-century type remained in use throughout this period, but Adam developed his own style with solid back-plates, rounded or oval, and with typical Adelphi details in their designs. The round 'ring' design shown in the photograph of the china-cabinet on page 101, which was much used on Louis Seize furniture, was especially popular with the Hepplewhite and Sheraton schools, and Sheraton also favoured the rather large flat oval plate. In general in Hepplewhite and Sheraton handles more attention is paid to prettiness than to strength. In rare cases they are not only flimsy but are silver-plated.

The lion's mask and ring handle which came into fashion in the last decade of the century is shown in the photograph of a Sheraton wine-cooler on page 118.

CHAPTER 14

The Genuine and the Not-so-Genuine

PREVIOUS chapters have been concerned with the characteristics of style and detail which enable a collector to give at any rate an approximate date to a given piece of Period furniture. The question which remains is how to tell whether the chair or table or mirror is or is not what it is claimed to be.

The student, and particularly the would-be purchaser, of an 'antique' wants to know whether it is in all respects genuine, or is a reproduction, or has been put together by combining fragments of genuine pieces, or is in the main genuine but has been 'improved' by the addition of decoration or other features in order to enhance its sale-value. Indeed, even if there has been no element of intentional deception, a Period piece may well have been repaired or had parts (such as the feet) replaced during the course of the years, and a buyer is entitled to know, and should endeavour to know, precisely what he is buying.

Obviously these questions open up a big subject. It is clear that the knowledge of the expert who is called upon to pronounce whether a given piece is in all respects genuine, must be very wide. In a particular case he may require to know the methods of construction employed in building an oak chest of the 17th century, or the detailed changes in the style of marquetry between the Restoration and the later years of Queen Anne, or the method of polishing used in the 18th century, or even the type of plane or other tools employed at a particular period. Many collectors and well-known dealers have endeavoured to impart to the readers of their books advice and hints derived from their long experience in handling all types of furniture, genuine and not-so-genuine, but they are confronted by the difficulty that this is a subject on which the written word and the photograph cannot be an adequate substitute for experience in seeing and handling the real thing.

This book has been written for the novice, and does not pretend to do more than attempt to indicate how he can best set about acquiring the necessary experience and the precautions which he would be wise to take in order to guard against deception.

A most important piece of advice centres round the term 'patina'. This is a term which was applied originally to antique bronzes, and refers to the particular soft bloom that accrues to the surface of the old bronze as a result of exposure to the atmosphere and friction through the centuries. In the case of furniture it is a convenient short expression for a particular kind of surface-condition. The oak of the late Tudor and Jacobean periods was normally oiled in the first instance, then treated with beeswax and turpentine and finally polished again and again. The walnut and mahogany of the 18th century was also carefully polished. The method described by Sheraton as in general use for plain cabinet-work was to apply linseed oil, allow a day or two for it to dry and then to rub with powdered brickdust. In all cases the result of the old treatment, in combination with the effect of time, is the mellow glow which is called 'patina'. It is a fact that this particular appearance is unmistakable when it is present in the case of old oak, and is only less so in the other woods, if they have not been gilded or painted over or treated by a later polishing process. The 'French polishing' with spirit polish introduced in the 19th century does not give the same result. Under the latter process mahogany, for example, was treated with bichromate of potash as part of the method and acquired a definitely red tint (in fact any shade of red desired) whereas mahogany of the 18th century has a golden brown hue if the condition arising from the original polishing has not been destroyed; but, apart from colour, the surface appearance given by 'French polishing' is not the same. The importance of being able to recognise the old wood in its 'patinated' condition can hardly, therefore, be exaggerated; and the first question for the novice is what practical steps he should take to gain this experience.

There is only one answer to that question. The first essential for all students of 'Period' furniture is to go and look at undoubted examples which have not been subjected to modern polishing. These can be studied in public collections and also in the stocks of the first-class dealers. The appearance given to the wood by its original polishing and the lapse of one or two centuries cannot be exactly reproduced by other methods, and its recognition is a weapon of the first importance in the armoury of the collector. Nor is it only this recognition of surface-condition that is learnt by inspection of undoubted examples of 'right' pieces. In the case of old oak, at any rate, many details of the old methods of construction are visible, and in the case of 18th century furniture, the finish given to details of the work by fine craftsmanship (both on the outside and the inside of the model) can be observed and noted, and the trained eye will be quick to discern inferior work.

It may be objected that some old oak was not polished originally and does not possess this patina, and that it would be fairly easy to build up a piece of oak furniture out of pieces of genuine old wood which have been suitably 'weathered'. This is true; and it may be added that, assuming fraudulent intent, it would also not be difficult to use the correct old methods of construction in producing the 'fake'. Many of the 'hints' that have been given by writers are concerned with this subject of the tricks of the trade that are said to be practised, and indeed are practised, by the unscrupulous type of seller, and it is only fair to point out that such tricks find no favour with reputable firms. At the same time it is a common foible of human nature to try to pick up a genuine piece 'for a song' in the shop of the small dealer in miscellaneous 'antiques', and if the collector chooses to rely on his judgment in such a case, it can only be said that, in the absence of patina, a piece made out of genuine old oak by the old methods of construction may be very difficult to judge; and the novice would be well advised to require the patinated condition in any 'old oak' which he proposes to purchase.

There can be no doubt that the study of original pieces is the best protection against deception. If the effect of time and wear on old wood is carefully observed, it is not easy to be deceived by any staining or other treatment of modern wood and the outright reproduction should be recognised in most cases without difficulty; but there are other important pieces of advice which the collector should note. For example, the point has often been made that carving in the old days had more 'life' than is likely to be found in an imitation. The meaning of this is that the imitator is following a set pattern and is likely to produce it mechanically. The imitation is likely to be even and regular, even if it is not lacking in the sharpness of definition that the craftsman of the old days gave to his work. The original carver was interpreting a design with a certain amount of freedom, and little irregularities occur which are avoided in the mechanical process of copying. This is one valuable point to observe in the genuine old work, and a second is the fact that in 'Period' times the maker was inclined to be prodigal of wood. In the 18th century very thick blocks of wood were used in order to allow for the curve in a chair-back or arm, and a great deal of wood was 'cut to waste'. In an imitation it is more than probable that economy in material will make itself shown. The same tendency to be economical of wood can also be observed in a modern copy of carved decoration, the result being a somewhat cramped and flatter effect than is gained by the old methods. It is also worth noting that a chair or settee made in solid walnut will be noticeably lighter than an old piece if it is made of modern wood; and that panels of modern veneer are most unlikely to show the fine figure that was the chief point in their selection in the furniture of the old days.

In other words, when the novice is advised to study 'the real thing' as a protection against being deceived by imitations, surface-condition is by no means the sole test. In early walnut furniture, for example, the original surface condition is often lacking and the collector has to fall back on the cumulative evidence of all those considerations which the expert brings into play in judging whether a piece of furniture is 'right'. Possibly the expert himself could not precisely analyse the 'instinct' which results from his long experience, but it certainly includes a critical appreciation of design, proportion, construction and workmanship for which the study of the genuine article is the best school.

A subject more difficult than the complete imitation is that of repairs, alterations and 'improvements'. Much old furniture has been repaired, and in other cases parts that have worn out have been replaced with no intention to deceive. These are legitimate restorations; but there is also the case where a more or less plain 'carcase' has been 'improved' with the dishonest purpose of adding to its market value. In the case of the legitimate repairs and alterations, the novice should remember that he is entitled to know precisely what he is buying, and it is no reflection on the seller if he examines a piece inside as well as out. The practical application of this precaution might be illustrated by the case of a William and Mary secretaire of the type shown on page 46. Sometimes these models had feet of the rectangular bracket type, but normally they stood on round bun-shaped feet of the Stuart fashion, and in some cases the original feet, which wore out rather easily, have been replaced by the bracket type, which became normal in the 18th century. The 'bun' foot was fastened on by means of a circular hole in the framework at the bottom of the model, and if the particular specimen has had its feet replaced the original holes will be still present. The facts on this point can be ascertained very simply by removing the lowest drawer and inspecting the framework at the corners underneath. The seller himself may be unaware of a replacement of this type, but it effects the value of the price. It is hardly necessary to say that the more that the amateur can learn about the old methods of construction, the better. There are dealers who are quite willing to allow visitors to their repair shops, and more knowledge can be acquired in this way than by the study of written details.

The fraudulent 'improvement' of an original piece is, of course, far more difficult because any new work will be disguised. If a table or chair or cabinet has been 'glorified' in order that it may command a considerable sum of money, it is unlikely that the perpetrator of the fraud will commit elementary mistakes. The work may be done with great skill and a great deal of knowledge and artistry, for, while it is true that this type of alteration and adornment is very often expensive to put into practice, it aims at conferring an enhanced value which will more than compensate for the expense. Here there is added point in the advice that examination should not be confined to the outward and immediately visible parts of a piece of furniture. If the 'improver' has added mouldings or carving or a strip of fret decoration to the face of a cabinet, he will probably have taken great pains to ensure that there is no crudeness about the added work, such as raw edges left by the saw in the cutting of a fret. The artist in this type of work is well aware that the fine craftsmen of the 18th century took infinite care in the finish of their mouldings, panels and detailed work generally. In judging the outside the potential buyer cannot rely on the assistance of a 'lapse' in workmanship; but it is always possible that less trouble may have been taken with those parts of a model which will not be seen except by a thorough examination. If the operations of the 'improver' affect the inside of a drawer, he may not have taken the necessary care over the finish of the dove-tailing, and, similarly, any alterations to the back-boarding may have received less attention. At any rate a thorough examination is a precaution that should always be taken, and if any modern work at all is detected on the 'unseen' portions (which in a given case may be a quite legitimate repair) the examination has been useful in inducing a more careful inspection of the rest of the piece and particularly of those features without which it would have been of far smaller value.

Two comparatively common forms of embellishment are the insertion of inlaid designs in mahogany furniture of the Sheraton era, and the addition of modern painting to a satinwood panel. These are relatively common because they are comparatively easy to add, and in both cases the appearance of age can be more or less faithfully reproduced. In the former case it is worth while remembering that Sheraton and his contemporaries relied very largely on the beauty of the wood which they used and did not overload it with inlaid decoration. As regards the inlay itself, modern inlaid designs have, to the eye of the expert, a machine-made appearance as compared with the real thing and a study of original work can give this experience. As to modern painting on satinwood, one well-known expert (Mr. Frederick Litchfield) went so far as to record his opinion some years ago that it is generally so inferior that it can be detected by any 'intelligent amateur'. But it can only be so detected as a result of careful study of original examples.

Probably the greatest difficulty is the *old* copy which was made without any idea of deceiving. Very fine copies of Period mahogany were made by good craftsmen during the Victorian era which were either frankly reproductions or old pieces ordered for making up gaps in genuine sets. These copies were made at a time when economy in wood was not necessary and standards of craftsmanship were high, and, when they were executed with great skill, they fall into the 'very difficult' class where the experience of the advanced expert is necessary.

Other very difficult subjects are gilded furniture, and old lacquer. The outward appearance of old gilding can be imitated very cleverly. The carved and gilded 'Chippendale' mirror, for example, has been extensively reproduced with great skill. Again, in the case of lacquer, the judgment whether in a doubtful case it is English or oriental, or whether it is early 18th century or later, calls for specialist knowledge. In both cases the amateur would be well advised not to rely on his own judgment.

The question is often asked whether copies of Period furniture in oak, walnut or mahogany can be made today so skilfully that advanced students would probably be deceived by them. The answer is that such copies *can* be produced provided that the wood is old wood and that the old methods of construction and polishing are employed. Their production demands, however, great skill in craftsmanship, much knowledge and a high degree of artistry; and they can only be produced at considerable expense. Copies of this quality would probably be made by reputable firms who sell them as copies. They are far removed from ordinary reproductions.

While the range of the knowledge on which the connoisseur or the professional expert relies is certainly extensive, the novice who aims at the collection of Period pieces of good average quality should not be discouraged by that fact, nor by the statement, so often heard, that the expert operates by a mysterious 'instinct'. The 'instinct' which the first-class expert develops is a composite thing. It is born partly of accumulated experience and partly, no doubt, of an 'artistic flair'. The first result of his experience is that he is able, in a doubtful case, to know immediately where to look for the signs of the 'not-so-genuine'. His 'flair' renders him quick to recognise faults in line, proportion, and decoration. Experience can be acquired by taking pains. The word 'flair' is usually used in the sense of a natural, inborn artistic perception. When people say of a person that he has a natural flair for a subject such as old furniture, they mean that the fortunate person in question possesses an eye for the work of an artist. Such an 'eye' does not tell its possessor that a chair is old in the sense of being a Period piece, for that requires some acquired knowledge, but it does tell him that it is the work of an artist. There are qualities of beauty which his eye did not need to be trained specially to perceive and appreciate. Fortunately for the 'man in the street', this 'eye', like experience, can be acquired; but there is no way of acquiring it other than in the study of the work of fine designers and craftsmen who have themselves possessed a strong artistic sense. In fine, the very real difficulty of the subject of the 'not-so-genuine' is not of a kind that should deter the amateur as requiring some super-sense to which he cannot aspire; but it does call for study and for the development of the artistic taste which the novice may be presumed to possess if he has any leaning for 'Period' furniture at all.

In the end, the best practical advice that can be given, in writing, to would-be collectors of old English furniture can probably be reduced to three main points. The first is that the novice should go and look for himself at examples of Period furniture which are genuine beyond any doubt. The second is that he should make use of any opportunity to acquaint himself with actual workshop methods. The third is to buy always from accredited dealers. An accredited dealer will provide, on request, a written description of the goods that he sells.

The study of this subject is worth while; for the training of the eye to appreciate and demand quality in design and workmanship is not only the best criterion for the collector, but is a contribution to the culture of the country. Those who are interested in the connection between the aesthetic appreciation of old English furniture and the question of England regaining the leading position which the country once held in this field, will find the subject discussed in a practical way in the report of the official Working Party on Furniture, which was published in 1946.

As Mr. Sacheverell Sitwell has written in reference to architecture, "It is by taking the past as an example but not copying it, that we shape the future."

Postscript (1959)

THE following notes correct or amplify statements made in the text.

Pages 20 to 22 and 26.

Modern research has shown that the terms 'court cupboard' and 'buffet' have been misapplied in the past. In the 16th century the court cupboard was a piece of furniture with open tiers such as is pictured on page 20 where it is called a buffet. It was literally a cup-board; that is to say, it provided boards for the display of cups or other pieces of plate or pewter. The piece of furniture which possesses doors and has been called a court cupboard was described as a 'press'.

Page 24.

The statement that fixed upholstery was unknown in the second half of the 16th century was not intended to contradict the undoubted fact that long before that date there were chairs with frames of beech covered all over with fabric nailed on to the wood.

Page 45.

The implication that the use of stretchers on pieces having cabriole legs was exceptional in the reign of Queen Anne does not apply to chairs. It was only when the cabriole leg was developed in its perfected form that stretchers were discarded for the cabriole-leg chair.

Page 132.

Matthias Lock. Lock and Copeland (or Copland) are best known as the designers of many plates in Chippendale's *Director*.

Page 134.

William Vile and John Cobb. The superlative quality of the work of Vile and Cobb is proved by the furniture made for the Court between 1760 and 1764.

Index